Advance praise for

Guide to Sea Kayaking in Central and Northern California

"From detailed site descriptions to practiced planning advice [this book] is a Northern California sea kayaker's classic. Throw this book in your cockpit and go!"
—Eugene Buchanan, Publisher, *Paddler* magazine

"This real-world guide provides exacting detail and thorough coverage of one of the world's most spectacular coastlines. Don't paddle there without it."
—Bryan Chitwood, Editor, *Canoe & Kayak* magazine

"The coast of California has some spectacular scenery, but it is not a place for the uninformed paddler. . . . Roger Schumann and Jan Shriner have both the experience to know what skills are required to paddle the more demanding stretches of the coast and . . . a knack for matching paddlers of various abilities with appropriate challenges. In [this book] paddlers of all abilities will find rewarding outings that will be well matched to their skills."

—Chris Cunningham, *Sea Kayaker* magazine

Help Us Keep This Guide Up to Date

Every effort has been made by the authors and editors to make this guide as accurate and useful as possible. However, many things can change after a guide is published—establishments close, phone numbers change, facilities come under new management, and so on.

We would love to hear from you concerning your experiences with this guide and how you feel it could be made better and kept up to date. While we may not be able to respond to all comments and suggestions, we'll take them to heart and we'll also make certain to share them with the authors. Please send your comments and suggestions to the following address:

The Globe Pequot Press

Reader Response/Editorial Department

P.O. Box 480

Guilford, CT 06437

Or you may e-mail us at:

editorial@globe-pequot.com

Thanks for your input, and happy travels!

Regional Sea Kayaking Series

Guide to Sea Kayaking in Central and Northern California

The Best Day Trips and Tours from the Lost Coast to Morro Bay

by

Roger Schumann and Jan Shriner

The Globe Pequot Press

Guilford, Connecticut

Cover design: Adam Schwartzman
Text design: Casey Shain
Cover photograph: Roger Schumann
Maps by: Mary Ballachino
Interior photos on pages 140–41, 157, and 166 by Art Today.com. All others by Roger Schumann and Jan Shriner.

Library of Congress Cataloging-in-Publication Data

Schumann, Roger.
    Guide to sea kayaking in Central and Northern
    California : the best day trips and tours from the Lost Coast to Morro
    Bay / by Roger Schumann and Jan
    Shriner. — 1st ed.
        p.   cm. (Regional Sea Kayaking series)
        Includes bibliographical references (p.) and
    index.
        ISBN 0-7627-0382-2
        1. Sea kayaking—California—Guidebooks.   2.
    California—Guidebooks.   I. Shriner, Jan.   II. Title.   III. Series.
    GV788.5.S38   1999
    797.1'224'09794—DC21   98-51686
                                  CIP

Manufactured in the United States of America
First Edition/Second Printing

To my mom, Lorraine Schumann, who now rests "at home in the sea," for her *undying* encouragement. And to my dad, Robert Schumann, who passes down his love for the sea as surely as his blue eyes, who taught me to catch waves on a boogie board practically since before I could walk, and who's still "boogying," last time we checked, at seventy-eight years young.

—Roger Schumann

To my family, especially my parents for nurturing my love of the water and the outdoors, my brothers for their comradery and acceptance of my adventures, and my grandparents, aunts, uncles, in-laws, cousins, nephews, and niece for sharing their exuberance and laughter.

—Jan Shriner

Cape Mendocino

■ SHELTER COVE

1

Lost
Coast

2

Sinkyone
Wilderness

3 ■ MENDOCINO

5 4 ■ BIG RIVER

6

Point Arena

Russian River

7

8

9

Cordel Banks
National Marine Sanctuary

10

11

12

Point Reyes

13

14

15 16

17

Gulf of the Farralones
National Marine Sanctuary

18

19

■ SAN FRANCISCO

San Francisco
Bay

20 21

PACIFIC

HALF MOON BAY

24

OCEAN

SAN JOSE ■

22

23

25

■ SANTA CRUZ

26 27

Monterey
Bay

28 29

31 30

■ MONTEREY

32

Salinas River

33

Monterey Bay National Marine Sanctuary

34 ■ BIG SUR

Ventana
Wilderness

35

N

36 ■ SAN SIMEON

0   20   40   60

miles

37

Morro
Bay

38

39

■ SAN LUIS
OBISPO

40

Contents

Acknowledgments

We are indebted to many without whose help, encouragement, and friendship this book would not have been written. Muchas gracias to Kate McLain and "Tomales" Tom Shores at Blue Waters Kayaking for freely sharing their local expertise in and around Tomales Bay and for taking the time to read over that section and make helpful suggestions. A special thanks to Tom for also joining us on several scouting expeditions, and for being Roger's big-water paddling buddy (those memorable moments amid the fury of a Mendocino gale, during a big spring ebb at South Tower, on the river, and many others, along with your friendship, mean more to me than perhaps you realize.)

We'd also like to thank the "A Team," Alicia and Renie Borowski, Dan Geiszler, Robert Zurowski, Bill Long, and Lynda Koch, for suggesting and joining all those open-coast exploratories over the years, especially the ones along Big Sur and the Lost Coast. Thanks to Lynda, along with Mary Lacour and Buck Johnson, for teaching classes for one of us, allowing the other to stay home to work on this book. Thanks to our other comrades at arms, Dean Partlow, Lisa Marrack, Mike McNulty, and others at Monterey Bay Kayaks for their friendship and professionalism, which has encouraged us through the years. Thanks too, to owner Jeff Schrock for his expertise in patching all those holes Roger manages to put in our boats. Thanks to Chris Cunningham at *Sea Kayaker* magazine for publishing all those articles and for passing Roger's name on to our editor, Laura Strom, at Globe Pequot Press when she was looking for a local author. Thanks to Laura for her patience in answering all those endless questions of first-time authors. Thanks to Lucia Orlando, at the UC Santa Cruz library map room for locating countless maps and then putting them all away; Drew at Bay Photo for being friendly, remembering our names, and always having our photos ready on time; Sandra Allen for refereeing the inevitable disagreements between coauthors; and Tim Greenstreet for Rolfing Jan into even better shape. Thanks to Robin for her letter of encouragement that arrived at precisely the right moment; to Lorilee and Denny for their constant encouragement, for scouting Morro Bay with us, and for all the fine times on the water and off; and to Lahna and family for sharing a family ski trip that recharged our batteries before the big push. A big gracias to Al G. for bringing the final maps to Baja for us to proof. And thanks to all of the customers of Eskape Sea Kayaking who have been looking for just such a guidebook and who support us at many levels to follow our dreams.

Map Legend

WATER

main route

Alternate route

launch site

8 buoy marker

marsh

visible rocks

submerged rocks

waves

LAND

hills

roads

trail

railroad

developed area/city

house

building

campground

P parking

cliffs

mud/tidal flats

Paddling the Pacific Coast

Renowned for its world-class scenery, the coastline of Central and Northern California spans three of the nation's twelve National Marine Sanctuaries, two wilderness areas, and one National Seashore. It's no accident this area has received so much protection—it is among the most spectacular and wildlife-rich marine habitats on the planet—and it's no accident we feature it here. Although there are literally hundreds of lakes, rivers, and marshes to paddle farther inland, when we were asked to write a book of "best trips" in this region, our thoughts naturally drifted to the coast. Although we also include a handful of the area's more peaceful and scenic lakes and rivers, by far the best paddling in the state is on salt water—from the quiet, bird-filled estuaries and protected bays to the exposed headlands of the open Pacific.

Best known for the rugged beauty of its wave-sculpted cliffs, the California coast is perhaps not the sort of placid shoreline many sea kayakers typically think of when it comes to dropping their boats in the water. But tucked away along these craggy shores are pockets of glassy water even Roger's sister, Lorilee, wouldn't hesitate to paddle. Lorilee is, in fact, a fairly accomplished if somewhat cautious paddler. Preferring protected waters, her thrills are simple: drifting past shorebirds that stalk the mudflats of Morro Bay, sneaking through the maze of salt marsh channels that fringe Elkhorn Slough, and camping on a deserted beach in the backwaters of Point Reyes National Seashore.

But she's also drawn like salmon smolt to the open sea. Vast horizons open up to any paddler willing to leave the security of the sloughs and harbors, and not all of them are limited to advanced rough-water kayakers. Many sheltered coves offer safe launching beaches with access to miles of intermediate paddling, so Lorilee has been practicing her surf landings and expanding her vistas. The amount of protected water is limited in our area, however, so advanced skills are the key to the best of the best: the remote "wilderness" beaches and sea caves that are inaccessible save by sea in a small boat seaworthy and maneuverable enough to negotiate surf zones and rock gardens.

This book is about exploring both the swimming-pool-calm backwaters as well as venturing out along the open coast. Routes described start with the famed Lost Coast of Mendocino County and sweep southward with the prevailing winds past the Point Reyes National Seashore, San Francisco Bay, the Monterey Bay National Marine Sanctuary and Big Sur coast, and on to Morro Bay in San Luis Obispo County. Most of the forty routes covered are day trips, giving options for beginner, intermediate, and advanced paddlers, so that *well over a hundred route alternatives exist.* Although camping is limited, we've included places where overnight trips are possible. Roger also drops in his passion for kayak surfing and rock gardens, mentioning many surfing and rough-water play spots.

Because a number of other books on the market deal specifically with teaching basic paddling techniques like strokes and rescues, we haven't attempted to cover them here. However, we do include a section on trip planning and water safety as they pertain to local hazards and an appendix with recommendations for skills books. However, since reading is no substitute for competent professional instruction, we've also included an appendix of local paddling schools. With a little time in the cockpit and some training, much of this amazing watery wonderland can be yours to explore.

Trip Planning, Water Safety, & Sea Sense

In recent years the sea kayaking industry has done a very good job of promoting the ease and accessibility of the sport—sometimes too good. It's true, practically anyone can enjoy kayaking. Modern boats are so user friendly that it's easy for people to hop on and go ... and get in over their heads. Making the boat go forward is the easy part. Picking a route that's compatible with your type of kayak, skill level, and conditions on the day you go out takes experience and something we call "sea sense." More art than science, sea sense takes time and experience to develop. Those with strong water backgrounds, sailors and surfers for example, may be ahead of the game, but they will still need to learn the limitations of this new craft. This is why we strongly recommend taking professional lessons at each level of your development and paddling with partners who know the area and are more skilled than you when exploring new places. We also suggest that the book *Deep Trouble* (see appendix A), a compilation of accident reports from *Sea Kayaker* magazine, should be considered mandatory reading by every kayaker: There is much to be learned from the mistakes of others.

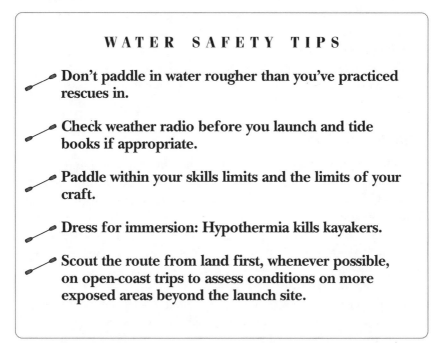

WATER SAFETY TIPS

- **Don't paddle in water rougher than you've practiced rescues in.**

- **Check weather radio before you launch and tide books if appropriate.**

- **Paddle within your skills limits and the limits of your craft.**

- **Dress for immersion: Hypothermia kills kayakers.**

- **Scout the route from land first, whenever possible, on open-coast trips to assess conditions on more exposed areas beyond the launch site.**

Hypothermia—Dress for Immersion

Statistically speaking, hypothermia is a sea kayaker's number one safety concern, accounting for the vast majority of kayaking accidents and fatalities. And our area is no exception. Most routes in the book are considered cold-water paddling environments because water temperatures generally hover in the 50s year-round. Some estuaries, rivers, or reservoirs may warm up during the summer, but the open coast rarely does. The savvy paddler's catch phrase, "Dress for immersion," implies dressing for the water temperature not the air temperature. Assume you will end up in the water and dress accordingly—wear a wet or dry suit that will keep you warm or dry if you get wet. If you get hot, it's much easier to cool down around water than it is to warm back up if you get cold. For safety we always carry a spare change of warm clothes in a waterproof dry bag, and typically we change into dry shirts when we stop for lunch and the cool breeze starts to blow. A warm cap is especially helpful—it takes up little space, and you lose most of your body heat from your head. Around cold water, they say, "Cotton kills," so all clothing that you wear on the water should be safe for immersion—wet suits, both neoprene and the newer laminated fabric wet suits made of Thermal Stretch, or dry suits. If you are not already familiar with the stages and effects of hypothermia, do yourself a favor and find out. Any kayak technique manual worth its salt will deal extensively with the subject.

Rescues & Reentries

The majority of kayaking accidents have a common theme: People start out in beginner areas, conditions change beyond their skill level, they capsize in bodies of water colder than 60 degrees (often without wet suit or life jacket); are unable to get back into their boats because they don't have the proper rescue gear or don't know how to use it, and then become hypothermic. People lose body heat five times faster when wet, but *twenty-five times faster when submerged!* So to combat hypothermia, we stress practicing rescues in all our classes. Instead of the term rescue, however, which connotes panic and being a victim, we prefer the more modern term reentry because it's calmer, more in control: You've fallen out of your boat, so you don't need to call the Coast Guard, you just need to climb back aboard. Our two favorite reentries for closed-cockpit kayaks—what we consider the bread-and-butter minimum skills—are the "paddle float self-rescue" and the "T rescue." If you don't know what these two techniques are, we recommend you don't venture farther from shore than you would wade until you've taken a lesson. Accident reports are full of those who thought they could simply climb back into their (now swamped and even less stable) kayaks or "just swim to shore." (Those on open-top kayaks should also be comfortable scrambling back aboard in a variety of conditions.) Then practice. Reentry skills get rusty quickly, so it's a good idea to practice every time you paddle. We also have our students practice simulated rough-water reentries to get comfortable getting back into their boats in the type of choppy conditions they're likely to capsize in. To practice this, find an impish friend who will enjoy trying to capsize you by bouncing on and twisting your bow while you're trying to reenter. This is an exercise in tough love, so show no mercy when you return the favor. Those with solid rescue skills rarely end up in accident reports, so remember the Golden Rule: *Don't paddle in waer that might get rougher than you've practiced rescues in.*

Boats & Gear

Although many routes in the book are appropriate for a variety of boats—open-deck kayaks, so-called recreational day-touring or compact kayaks, and even canoes—the book is written primarily with full-length, closed-deck sea-touring kayaks in mind, typically those in the 14- to 18-foot range and not more than 25 inches wide, generally with bulkheads and hatches fore and aft. We find these boats are the most efficient, seaworthy, and versatile. Open-deck kayaks will also work on most routes and have the advantage of being more affordable and more user-friendly for beginners. Most standard sit-on-tops, however, are less efficient, especially in wind, so overall mileage covered may be limited. The popular "day-touring" and compact kayaks that are less than 13 feet long and wider than 25 inches are not recommended beyond the "Beginner" segments of each route. Although these kayaks are loads of fun and very user friendly, they are typically designed only for calm-water locations. When capsized, their large, high-volume cockpits tend to flood with water, even if equipped with float bags, making them extremely difficult to rescue.

Whatever your craft, the Coast Guard requires that each paddler carry a wearable life jacket (a Type III Personal Floatation Device or PFD) on their boat; however, most drownings involve people *carrying* PFDs instead of *wearing* them. The idea is to think ahead and be prepared with intentionally redundant safety items. The following list is considered the standard minimum safety equipment.

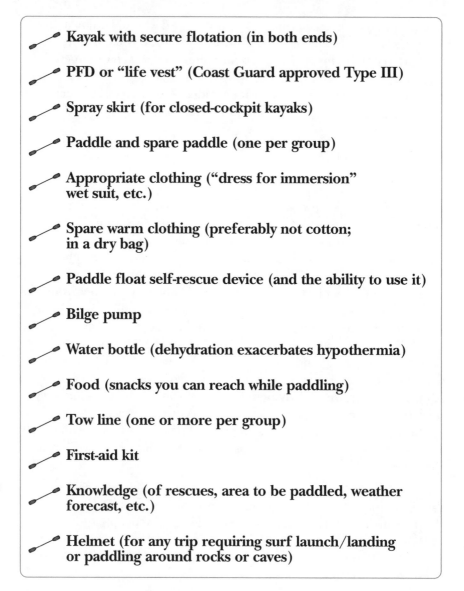

- Kayak with secure flotation (in both ends)

- PFD or "life vest" (Coast Guard approved Type III)

- Spray skirt (for closed-cockpit kayaks)

- Paddle and spare paddle (one per group)

- Appropriate clothing ("dress for immersion" wet suit, etc.)

- Spare warm clothing (preferably not cotton; in a dry bag)

- Paddle float self-rescue device (and the ability to use it)

- Bilge pump

- Water bottle (dehydration exacerbates hypothermia)

- Food (snacks you can reach while paddling)

- Tow line (one or more per group)

- First-aid kit

- Knowledge (of rescues, area to be paddled, weather forecast, etc.)

- Helmet (for any trip requiring surf launch/landing or paddling around rocks or caves)

Additional safety gear (depending on the difficulty of the trip, it may include tide and current tables, charts and maps, compass, flares, waterproof flashlight, weather radio, boat repair kit, VHF marine radio or cell phone, survival kit, etc.)

Weather—*The Pacific High, Northwest Winds, & Paddling in the Lee*

For those who learn to work around the weather, the central and north coast is blessed with a year-round paddling season. The main concept to understand about safely paddling this area is the prevailing northwesterly weather pattern and how it's affected by coastal topography. During most of the year (spring, summer, and fall), a stable high pressure system called the Pacific High parks off the California coast like a giant umbrella, sloughing storm systems north into Oregon and Washington. Largely responsible for the state's famous sunshine, the Pacific High also has a big affect on local winds. Because high pressure systems spin clockwise in the northern hemisphere, wind blows in off the ocean from out of the northwest, deflects off the coast range mountains, and follows the coastline southeastward. And since land heats faster than water—as the great inland valley, the San Joaquin, heats up each day with the rising sun—hot air rising over it creates a giant vacuum, drawing the cool, dense coastal air southward and inland with increasing velocity as the day heats up. (This atmospheric suction is why some kayakers claim the wind doesn't blow on the coast, it sucks.) By afternoon 15- to 25-knot northwesterlies are commonplace, even on lakes and sloughs well inland. This wind bends around out of the west, creating so-called gap winds, where it funnels through gaps in the coast range, such as through the Golden Gate and at the mouths of many rivers and sloughs.

The main problems with paddling in wind are that it slows progress if you're bucking it, it can push you where you don't want to go (for example, into cliffs, rocks, or boat channels), and it creates choppy seas and waves. As whitecaps begin to form around 10 knots or so, a paddler heading into the wind will be slowed by about 1 knot (1 nautical mile per hour, approximately 1.2 M.P.H.). Because most paddlers cruise at 3 or 4 knots, that can mean a significant loss in progress. A 15-knot headwind can knock your speed in half, and only the strongest paddlers can make crawling progress against 20 to 25 knots. As you tire, the wind can blow you off course or into hazardous conditions, so consider wind strength and direction when planning a trip. Another problem with wind is that it forms waves. The longer and stronger it blows, and the longer the *fetch*—or expanse—of open water it blows across, the choppier the seas become. Even on a lake. Where wind opposes a tidal

Paddling the Pacific Coast   -7-

current, steep breaking seas can form. On the open coast, ocean waves break on beaches, greatly complicating launching and landing (see Swell & Surf, page 10).

Tips for Paddling in the Wind

So what's all this mean to a kayaker? There are a few good ways to handle the wind. The first thing you want to do is buy a portable weather radio. One of the best $25 investments you can make for your comfort and safety, it broadcasts a continuous marine forecast, including wind and swell reports, that is updated every few hours. You can check it before you launch and periodically throughout the day. Those with Internet access can also find excellent marine weather sources, such as "Call of the Wind" and a NOAA forecast replete with maps, but these are not as portable as your trusty radio.

One way to avoid wind is to "time" your paddle: Leave early in the morning and get off the water before the wind starts blowing or try a short evening paddle after it has died. This is especially good advice for beginners. Note that when whitecaps begin to form, they should act as warning flags to novice paddlers.

Another way to dodge the wind is to paddle in the *lee*, the protected downwind side of points of land. On this coast that generally means the windy side faces north and the lee faces south. Most of our trips begin in the lee of points.

A popular strategy is to use the wind by paddling northward into it in the morning, then it'll be at your back for your return in the afternoon when you are likely to be tired. More advanced paddlers often run a shuttle, leaving a vehicle at a landing site to the south and paddling with the wind all day. Running a shuttle, however, creates logistical problems, the least of which are the time involved and remembering to bring your keys to the landing beach (don't laugh it happens with embarrassing regularity); the worst of which can include the inability to backtrack against the wind if conditions become too rough and finding yourself committed to completing a dangerous trip.

The final strategy is to simply plan to save some energy for the return trip, a common technique for paddling coastal rivers on which the last mile or so back to the launch site at the mouth often involves a slog into wind funneling upriver off the ocean. Using hills or banks as natural windbreaks can sometimes help in these situations.

Seasonal Weather Patterns

During winter time the Pacific High weakens and drifts southward, allowing storm tracts to hit the coast. Because winds spin counterclockwise around low pressure systems, southerly winds typically precede a storm front and should be a warning sign to off-season paddlers. These storms often send large swells to batter the coastline, making coastal touring difficult. Between storms, however, calm, sunny days in the mid 50s are not uncommon. With bird and gray whale migrations in full swing, paddling conditions are often quite good, even on the open coast, provided the swell is not up.

Spring is the unsettled season; the Pacific High battles with approaching storm fronts as it migrates northward and tries to become reestablished. Gusty northwest winds are common as well as occasional late-season storms. It may be cool and breezy one day, sunny and calm the next, and stormy the day after. Coastal kayakers need to choose their days carefully to avoid large swells from storms passing to the north, but experienced kayak surfers often enjoy the year's best and most consistent surfing. Conditions tend to settle down as the season progresses.

Summer brings fog to the coast, which typically burns off about the time the afternoon winds kick up. For days and weeks on end a common coastal forecast will call for morning fog, afternoon winds to 15 knots, and swells of 4 to 6 feet. As inland valleys swelter, the coast keeps its cool, with temperatures in the high 60s to low 70s.

Fall is the prime season, especially for coastal touring. Fog, wind, and swell often dwindle to naught, along with the summer beach traffic. Indian summer temperatures may soar into the 70s and 80s at the beach and the water temperature may reach the mid 60s.

Tides & Currents

Knowing how to read a tide book and *then checking the tides before you paddle* can be as important as checking the weather for nearly every route in this book. Especially in estuaries, sloughs, and coastal rivers, knowing the tide height and direction of currents can make the difference between catching a free ride on the currents, becoming mired in a mile-wide mudflat, or even getting washed out to sea. Getting caught in strong, ocean-going currents at the mouths of rivers and estuaries during an ebb (falling) tide is a common cause of boating accidents; it has already contributed to at least one kayaking fatality in our area. On the open coast where small pocket beaches at the base of cliffs can be rare as jewels, currents are generally negligible, but a high tide can cover the only launch beach for miles under a wash of breaking waves, and a low tide could expose dangerous rocks in the surf zone at your landing site. Only the lake routes are exempt from tidal influences (but not from seasonal fluctuations in water level).

In California we have two highs and two lows each day, which means that every six hours (give or take an hour or so) the tide rises to high, and six hours later it falls to low. In this cycle one of the highs is higher and one of the lows is lower. Tide height is measured from the mean level of the lower low at 0.0 feet, and in our area typically it fluctuates within a 6-foot range of an average water level of around 3 feet. Lunar phases affect this range, with more extreme tides occurring every two weeks around the full and new moon. In other words a small tide change for our area may only be from a 4- or 5-foot high to a 1- or 2-foot low, while larger changes typically range from more than 6 feet to *minus tides* of negative 1 foot.

The larger the tide range on a given day, the stronger the currents will be in narrow bodies of water during ebb (falling) and flood (rising) tides. San Francisco Bay is the only location in our area with actual current charts (widely available at kayak and sailing shops), showing direction and strength of currents. For other areas you'll need to extrapolate current strength from tide range and personal experience. We also suggest taking a "Tides and Currents" class from one of several Bay Area outfitters (see appendix B) to learn about hazards such as tide rips and skills such as eddy hopping as well as how to interpret tide and current logs.

Swell & Surf

Unlike many popular kayaking areas, such as the Pacific Northwest and much of the East Coast, which have literally hundreds of miles of protected inland passages, sheltered waters in our area are limited. This means that getting into the better paddling areas often means getting through the surf zone. Fortunately there are many protected beaches and many days of small surf, so that given a little training, along with good site selection and timing, most paddlers can enjoy the ocean environment.

Since ocean swells, like the wind, typically approach our coast from the northwest, south-facing beaches in the lee of points tend to have the best protection. Therefore checking the marine weather forecast for the size and direction of the swell is an important part of any coastal tour. Expect swells approaching from the west or south to bring rougher conditions, and swells over 6 feet on exposed (west or northwest-facing) beaches to challenge even advanced paddlers.

As swells reach the shallow bottom of a beach, they become breaking waves or surf, and handling a sea kayak in surf can be difficult at first. We highly recommend taking at least one surf zone class before challenging the waves and always wearing a helmet. Start small. Our rule of thumb for novice surf launches is that if the waves are over your head when you're sitting in your kayak, you are probably getting in *over your head*, meaning pick a different beach or a different day.

Be aware that some beaches, especially in the Santa Cruz area, do not allow kayaks or restrict their launch sites because of too many people in the water. Ask a local kayak store owner or lifeguard before unloading your boat. When landing or launching, it is important to stay well away from others in the water—swimmers, surfers, etc.—because an out-of-control kayak in the waves is a dangerous thing, and launch access could become further restricted if kayakers gain a reputation for running people over.

Once you gain good control in the surf, you may want to try kayak surfing. At first the best place to practice is well away from people, especially board surfers. Once a kayak broaches sideways on a wave and starts sidesurfing toward shore, it becomes an out-of-control "surf mower," 15 feet wide and plowing over anything in its path. As you gain more control, and this probably means a bombproof Eskimo roll for closed-deck kayakers, you may want to tackle better-known surf breaks. If so don't be a "Barney" or "kook": Please adhere to the long-standing rules of surf etiquette. To avoid collisions the first person on the wave, or the one closest to the break, gets the wave. Catch waves with no one else on them, and especially don't "drop in" and catch a wave that is occupied. Even with expert surfing skills, we generally stay off on the shoulders of the waves and well away from the board surfers. Dropping in on or running over surfers in some spots will probably get you cussed out or even physically threatened. Occasionally we've been cursed even when we were well away from the line up, but most surfers are accepting when they see you understand the rules, are in control of your craft, and present no hazard.

Open-Coast Paddling

Once through the surf you'll find some of the finest paddling in our area—as well as some of the most challenging—along the open coast. In some areas a short paddle around a headland will leave the parking lot and people far behind as you enter a coastal wilderness of isolated beaches and rugged solitude. The siren call of the open coast can be very alluring. However, it can also be alarming, depending on the skills and experience of the group and the conditions that day. Often coastal touring is more akin to white-water river paddling than sea kayaking, sharing similar thrills and hazards, while requiring the same level of rough-water paddling expertise and water-reading skill.

Exposure is a key consideration: If something goes awry—if the fog comes in, or the wind or swell comes up, or you get tired or hurt, or you break a paddle—are you five minutes or 5 miles from the nearest landing beach? Does that beach have access to a road, or is it sheer cliffs? Is the beach even a twenty-four-hour beach, or is it awash with surf at high tide like many? A million things can go wrong at sea and the greater your exposure, the less room for error.

The open coast can be as unforgiving as it is awesome, so we strongly recommend a conservative approach to any who dare sample its wonders. Stay in protected areas unless you have strong surf and rough-water rescue skills. Wear a helmet. Take an open-coast class. Paddle with experienced partners. Always check the marine weather report and choose a day with conditions well within your limits. Know where "bail out" beaches are, and scout them from land first if possible. Stay outside of rock-garden surf zones and caves unless you have a reliable Eskimo roll and advanced water-reading skills. (Remember, in many areas your paddling buddies will not be able to rescue you without endangering themselves.) And never, *never* underestimate the power of the sea—remember that waves breaking against rocks exert hundreds of pounds of pressure per square foot, and that kayakers in our area have already been injured or killed on the open coast. That some will ignore these warnings, no matter how emphatic, is something we regret. For those who do heed our advice, we offer the best of luck, for there are no guarantees and no ways to eliminate the risks entirely.

Basic Kayak Navigation

With few islands, crossings, or confusing passages in this area, following the shoreline for 5 or 10 miles in a day and recognizing landmarks with or without a map often works just fine. Instead of marine charts, which in our area tend to cover too much territory to be useful to kayakers, we often use topographic maps because they generally provide better detail. We especially like to photocopy sections of the map and laminate the pages to slip under the front deck bungies for use underway. The trick is to know what landmarks to look for while on the water, and what constitutes a major point versus another rock outcrop. The ability to navigate by chart and compass (and perhaps Global Positioning System [GPS]) can come in handy in the fog and could be essential on open-water crossings. The Coast Guard offers navigation courses, and some kayak shops in our area have classes that are more specific to kayakers. David Burch's *Fundamentals of Kayak Navigation* makes an excellent resource, but reading it cover to cover is probably less helpful than turning to it when you have a specific question.

Minimum Impact

As relatively new kids on the block, sea kayakers are in somewhat the same boat as mountain bikers were when that sport began to boom. There were no regulations at first, until a few screw-ups started cutting new trail, zooming past hikers, and ruining it for the rest of us. Soon bikes were banned in many areas. To prevent this from happening to kayakers, it's important to establish a reputation as a responsible user group. Otherwise we may find NO KAYAKING signs at our favorite launch beaches.

"No Flee" Wildlife Viewing & the Marine Mammal Protection Act

A major concern resource managers have with kayakers is their affect on wildlife. Designed as a hunting boat, the kayak is so stealthy and efficient at approaching wildlife living in or near the water that it's easy to get too close. Scaring seabirds off nests exposes eggs and chicks to predators. Flushing seals off haul outs disturbs their important "naps," when they are trying to warm up between hunting forays; it can also separate pups from mothers and pups sometimes get crushed in the stampede. We suggest adopting a "no flee" viewing ethic, that is, not getting close enough to cause animals to flee. Not only is this good wilderness etiquette, it's the law. In 1972 the Marine Mammal Protection Act was passed, prohibiting "harassment"—defined as any act causing animals to alter their natural behavior—and recommending that humans maintain a distance of 100 yards. Breaking this federal law carries a stiff penalty with fines up to $10,000. (Marine birds also enjoy protection under a different statute.) And in many areas, especially in state parks and wildlife refuges, rangers and visitors viewing animals from shore with high-powered binoculars will not hesitate to report an errant kayaker.

WILDLIFE VIEWING TIPS

With a little sensitivity and a good pair of binoculars, viewing marine wildlife in its natural habitat needn't disturb it. The main things to remember are to keep your distance and act disinterested. Like humans, animals too have "comfort zones" and don't like anyone crowding their personal space. On the open coast where animals are not used to people, even the 100 yards recommended by the Marine Mammal Protection Act may not be sufficient. In areas with kayak rentals like Elkhorn Slough or Cannery Row where animals are used to kayaks, 50 feet (a good three or four kayak lengths) is about as close as you should get. If a marine mammal lifts its head to look at you, or if a bird defecates and stretches its wings to prepare for flight, that's a sign they're feeling nervous and about to flee. Move away quietly while turning and looking in the other direction. This is where the "act disinterested" part comes in. Animals can tell when they're being stalked; they don't understand that you're only brandishing a camera. Heading straight toward, or looking directly at, any bird or animal will generally be construed as a threat, regardless of your intentions. Sometimes we even pretend to act wary, as if *we* were trying to avoid *them*. By approaching at a parallel angle and looking out of the corner of your eyes, you're less likely to spook them, and you'll enjoy better viewing. One final tip: Be quiet. Yelling, "Hey, dude, check out that otter!" at the top of your lungs is not the best way to alert your paddling partners. If you drift silently and pretend not to notice, animals tend to relax and let you view to your heart's content.

Pack It In, Pack It Out

This overused adage is obvious on the surface, but it applies to *all* our trash—even the "biodegradable." Beginning students sometimes ask if it's okay to toss an apple core on the launch beach at Elkhorn Slough, not realizing that maybe a hundred paddlers a week stop there, and that apple cores take a few weeks to break down. Besides the obvious aesthetic impact, introducing an outside food source changes the natural balance and can attract pests. Human waste is also an issue. In Tomales Bay kayak campers are now being asked to carry portable toilets. In general near salt water, the solution to pollution is dilution, so the best place to leave anything (from toothpaste spit to fire pits) is in the water or wet sand where the tides will "flush" it. Near freshwater, backcountry protocol recommends relieving yourself at least 100 feet from streams or lakes.

Other Access Issues

Respecting closed areas is another good way to avoid conflicts. Some areas are off limits to kayakers to protect sensitive wildlife habitat; others, to protect bathers at popular beaches or private property above the high-tide line. Kayakers need to be aware of these areas. During trip planning contact park rangers or local kayak shops to become educated on sensitive areas and access regulations. Learning about traffic patterns and etiquette before paddling around other boats also helps our reputation as competent boaters. Basically stay to the right, stay aware, and stay out of the way. *Sea lice* is a term other boaters use for kayakers whose lack of awareness makes them a navigational hazard. By educating themselves and minimizing their impact, kayakers can maximize their access and become a welcome addition to the marine environment.

How to Use This Book:
Guide to Route Descriptions

The following is an explanation of the various sections of each route description. Especially important are the definitions of our rating system and the skills and types of boat expected at the *Beginner, Intermediate,* and *Advanced* levels.

Route 31:

Monterey's Cannery Row to Point Piños & Beyond

This is the route number and area covered in the trip, followed by a one paragraph description—our attempt to capture the essence of what makes the route unique.

TRIP HIGHLIGHTS: Provides an at-a-glance list of the area's main attractions.

TRIP RATING: Not intended to replace good personal judgment and paddling experience, the trip rating suggestions are meant only as a general guideline to the level of skill recommended and distance involved for each route (or portion of the route). This assumes a typical summer weather forecast with prevailing wind (and swell, if applicable) coming out of the northwest and building in the afternoon. Paddlers may well need to adjust their plans during atypical conditions. Many normally protected coastal launch sites, for example, will lose some or all of that protection when swells approach out of the west or south.

Rating routes is problematic because sea conditions often vary drastically from day to day. Some areas can change from dead calm to deadly in a matter of hours, especially on the open coast. Even the most protected inland routes can become extremely challenging on a blustery afternoon. On the other hand, some open-coast areas that generally require advanced skills will sometimes be appropriate for beginners or intermediates on very calm days; however, we only recommend paddling such areas (as noted in the text) when accompanied by a more experienced paddler with the water reading skills to choose a conservative route—and the rescue skills to get you back in your boat if you capsize anyway.

Beginner: This part of the route is for someone with basic boat handling skills who is comfortable maneuvering on flatwater or light chop in winds to 10 knots. You've taken at least one class or have learned basic rescue techniques and are able to get back into your boat (or back on top of a sit-on-top) after a capsize. You understand the basics of local weather patterns and water safety, and you can read a tide book so that you don't get stuck in the mud. Most beginner sections are in enclosed estuaries, rivers, and lakes near shorelines, offering landing access in case conditions worsen. Surf is generally nonexistent or less than 1 foot, and currents are not more than 1 or 2 knots. In addition to touring kayaks and sit-on-tops, appropriate boats for this level may include recreational or compact kayaks and canoes.

Intermediate: This level is for those with enough skill and experience to handle choppy water comfortably in wind to 15 knots. You've probably taken a surf zone class and can launch and land through small surf, using side surfing and timing, and you might even have started kayak surfing. You have good braces, but you also practice rescues in open water and can recover from a capsize within two minutes in "real-life" conditions; you may be working on getting an Eskimo roll. Those paddling San Francisco Bay or other tidally influenced areas have a basic understanding of kayak navigation and tidal currents: ability to read chart, compass and tide logs, and to eddy hop. If paddling in coastal areas, you've done so with advanced paddlers to learn to avoid "boomers" and other hazards, and you have good sea sense, perhaps from your background in other ocean sports, for example, surfing, diving, or sail boarding. In areas we would label intermediate, you may launch through surf up to 3 feet, so helmets are strongly recommended. You may encounter ocean swell of 3 to 6 feet or currents to 3 knots and expect increased exposure to shorelines where landing access is limited, with 1 mile or more between beaches. Boat recommendations: Touring kayaks are suggested for day and overnight trips, but sit-on-tops may be okay for shorter sections. Recreational or compact kayaks and canoes are generally not appropriate or seaworthy enough for the rougher conditions you'll encounter.

Advanced: Not only are you comfortable in rough water, you probably enjoy it, going out of your way to play around in surf, rock gardens, and tide rips. You have a good Eskimo roll and solid bracing and rough-water rescue skills. You have a firm grasp of navigation, strong water reading skills, and a well-developed sea sense. Several of the advanced sections are the intermediate sections during rough conditions: when waves on the beach are 3 to 6 feet or more and wind is above 15 to 20 knots. Other advanced sections are remote and exposed, with several miles or more between landing beaches, or with beaches that require running a gauntlet of rocks in the surf zone. We've kept advanced-level route descriptions intentionally vague: Advanced paddlers will need little more than directions to the parking lot, while those needing more details (such as what type of boat is appropriate) might consider going with more experienced paddlers.

TRIP DURATION: Tells whether the route (or portions thereof) can be paddled in part of a day, will take a full day, and if it has overnight camping possibilities.

NAVIGATION AIDS: Gives the names of U.S. Geologic Survey topographical maps (and scale in minutes of latitude, either 7.5 or 15) as well as any marine charts useful for the route. Marine weather radio ("Wx radio") information tells which section(s) of the NOAA forecast to listen to along with the closest buoys. (see Trip Planning and Water Safety page 2).

TIDAL INFORMATION: Gives information regarding tide levels (such as "mudflats uncover at tides below 2 feet" or "beaches covered at high tide") and assumes you know how to read a tide book.

CAUTIONS: A list of hazards encountered en route (e.g., "boat traffic at harbor mouth, offshore winds, submerged rocks") that will also be noted in the mile-by-mile route description.

TRIP PLANNING: Tips to make the trip safer and easier; e.g., "paddle early to avoid the wind, and, on busy summer weekends, to find better parking."

LAUNCH SITE: Directions to the launch site, usually from Highway 1, as well as rest room facilities available, if any, and fees. Alternate launch sites also listed.

DIRECTIONS: A mile-by-mile route description listing **prominent landmarks** in bold type as noted on the maps, along with good landing beaches, interesting sites, cautions for hazards en route, and sidetrip options.

OTHER OPTIONS: Gives information on other good trips in the same area.

WHERE TO EAT & WHERE TO STAY: This section provides information on where to find food, lodging, and camping nearby.

The Lost Coast
& Mendocino

Route 1:

━━ ━━ ━━ ━━ ━━ ━━ ━━ ━━ ━━ ━━ ➤

Shelter Cove to Bear Harbor

Dramatic vistas of steep cliffs plunging to the sea from a 2,000-foot ridgeline make the Lost Coast among the most scenic paddling areas on the West Coast. Here Cape Mendocino—the westernmost point of land in the "Lower 48"—plows into the Pacific, awash in sea spray, like the bow of a giant ship. In the 40-mile lee of this massive cape are a handful of remote beaches where, under the right conditions, a skilled and adventurous paddler might make landfall. Although intermediate kayakers with good sea sense may enjoy short trips in the vicinity of Shelter Cove or Bear Harbor, the rest of this route can challenge even the most advanced coastal paddlers. The rewards, however, are great, as this remains the wildest stretch of seashore in the state.

TRIP HIGHLIGHTS: World-class coastal scenery, solitude, and excellent rock gardens.

TRIP RATING:

Beginner: 1 mile around Shelter Cove on days with no surf on the beach, little wind, and an advanced paddler in the lead. It's not very far, but it's quite a mile!

Intermediate: 1 mile around Shelter Cove in surf to 3 feet, wind to 15 knots, for those with previous coastal paddling experience. With the same calm conditions and an advanced paddler in the lead, 2 to 3 miles north from Shelter Cove (or from Bear Harbor) is possible; the entire 9 miles from Shelter Cove to Bear Harbor might also be possible, but it is not recommended due to the extreme exposure.

Advanced: 9 miles one way; shorter day trips possible from launch sites at either end. Strong coastal skills are required: rough-water paddling and rescue skills, water reading, and navigation. Not recommended in swells above 6–8 feet or winds above 20–25 knots.

TRIP DURATION: Part day, full day, or overnight.

NAVIGATION AIDS: *Trails of the Lost Coast: A Recreation Guide to King Range National Conservation Area and Sinkyone Wilderness State Park,* designed for hikers, it shows beaches and campsites but not the numerous offshore rocks. Map 39123-E1-TB-100: *Covelo* provides a good overview. Produced in a joint effort by the USGS and NOAA, it does an excellent job of showing and naming offshore reefs, rocks, and sea stacks. Its main drawbacks are that it misses the first 1 or 2 miles around Shelter Cove, shows no campsites, and the 1:100,000 scale is a bit small on detail. Wx radio: "Cape Mendocino to Point Arena"; buoys: Point Arena.

TIDAL INFORMATION: More landings possible on cliff-front beaches at low tide.

CAUTIONS: This coast is well known for fog, strong afternoon winds, and rough seas that can come in suddenly, so advanced seamanship is necessary to safely paddle here. The area is extremely exposed, with numerous offshore rocks and boomers but few good landing beaches. A weather radio is a must; unlike most cliffy coastal areas in the state, reception here is good throughout.

TRIP PLANNING: The best advice is to either be very conservative in paddling within the protection of Shelter Cove or to be very good at open-coast kayaking. Once you leave Shelter Cove, beaches are few, and the prevailing winds will be in your face if you turn around, so stay close to Shelter unless you are experienced. To avoid wind, paddle either early in the day (although fog could be a problem) or late afternoon after the wind has died. Small swell and low tide will be required to land on most beaches along the cliffs. If you don't have a second vehicle to leave at Bear Harbor, you can probably hitch a ride back to Shelter Cove, or you can arrange for a shuttle with Ed at Shelter Cove Campground (707) 986–7474. Save some energy for a hike at the end of the day—the trail from Bear Harbor to the parking lot is a good 0.5 mile. If planning to camp at Bear Harbor (or beyond), you'll need to pick up a camping permit from the Needle Rock Visitor Center.

LAUNCH SITE: To reach Shelter Cove from Highway 101 in Garberville, take the Redway exit and follow signs to Shelter Cove on Shelter Cove Road, a very scenic and twisting one hour drive. In Shelter Cove, follow signs to the boat ramp, down a steep hill to a protected beach. No fee. The landing site/alternate launch site at Bear Harbor can be reached directly from Shelter Cove Road via Briceland Road and Bear Harbor Road, or from Shelter Cove by following Chemise Mountain Road south.

DIRECTIONS:

START: Launch in the shelter of the stone jetty and head east and south along the coastline.

MILE 1.0: Point No Pass marks the end of the walking accessible beach and probably the end of the road for less-experienced paddlers. For the next 4 miles, a near-constant wall of cliffs prevents landings except on occasional low-tide beaches with steep shores and dumping surf. A profusion of nondescript points and countless offshore rocks makes navigation a challenge: It is difficult to tell where you are on the map, especially in the fog.

MILE 5.5: In the lee of (the second) **Point No Pass,** there are a few slightly larger and better-protected beaches, making this area among the best midway stopping points if you're ready to eat lunch or stretch your legs.

MILE 7.0: Jones Beach, an inviting mile-long stretch of sand at the foot of a coastal bench, is one of the longest beaches on this coast. A good place to land on calm days, it has less protection from surf than the beaches at Point No Pass. The marine terrace behind the beach is the first obvious landmark (but it could be difficult to spot in the fog). Look for the **Needle Rock Visitor Center** by a cluster of pines on the bluff about a mile farther down the coast.

MILE 9.5: High Tip, an obvious and aptly named landmark, is the 113-foot, cone-shaped spire at the end of the bluffs, where the coastline steepens again. Expert paddlers will find the scattering of sea stacks for the next 1 mile below the point among the more interesting and challenging rock gardens in the area.

MILE 11: To reach the beach at **Bear Harbor**, swing wide around the reef off the point at **Cluster Cone Rocks** and approach from the south, winding your way carefully between the submerged rocks and surf breaks to a fairly protected sand beach.

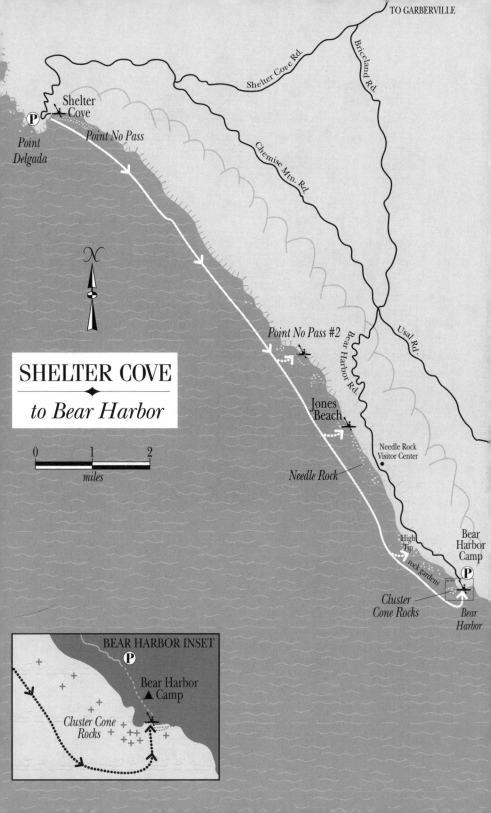

Lost Coast

Coast Route 1 is renowned as much for its scenic beauty as for being an engineering marvel. It winds steadily up the California coastline for hundreds of miles, hairpin curves clinging stubbornly to impossible cliffs, overlooking some of the finest ocean vistas on the planet. Then suddenly, somewhere below Cape Mendocino, it loses its way. The famous highway runs into one hundred miles of shoreline so steep and rugged, it turns tail and scampers miles inland. This is the Lost Coast, a region of dizzying verticality and supreme isolation. It's well known among savvy backpackers who've discovered what road builders long ago conceded, the region is best traversed on foot. Or is it? The Lost Coast Trail through Sinkyone Wilderness yo-yos up and down over a series of thousand-foot ridges, rigorous as it is beautiful. The route by sea is definitely shorter, but it is no less demanding. Beaches along the cliffs are few, steep and exposed, and tough to land on. There are just no easy ways around the Lost Coast, no shortcuts. Therein, for some, lies the attraction.

Where to Eat & Where to Stay

RESTAURANTS Fresh-caught fish and chips is the specialty at the *Shelter Cove Deli* (707–986–7474), along with burgers, made-to-order deli sandwiches and milkshakes. The deli is part of the *Shelter Cove RV Park and Campground* at the top of the hill from the boat ramp at 492 Machi Road. **LODGING** *Shelter Cove Beachcomber Inn*, a mile from the boat ramp, has rustic duplexes for $65 to $85 per night; (800) 718–4789. **CAMPING** *Shelter Cove RV Park and Campground* makes a convenient staging ground for a trip, although its closely packed sites are nothing special. They'll let you park your car there for free if you spend the night at Bear Harbor or continue down the coast. Call (707) 986–7474 for reservations.

Route 2:

■ ■ ■ ■ ■ ■ ■ ■ ■ ■ ■ ■ ■ ■ ■ ➤

Bear Harbor to Usal Beach & Beyond

Together with the previous 11-mile trip from Shelter Cove (Route 1), this 19-mile section of pristine coastline is one of the premier open-coast tours in the state, and one of the most challenging. Once you leave Bear Harbor, you are committed to a roadless, 8-mile section of cliffs and waves with few good landing beaches.

TRIP HIGHLIGHTS: World-class coastal scenery, kayak camping, solitude, and excellent rock gardens.

TRIP RATING:

Intermediate: 1–8-mile (round-trip) day trips north from Usal Beach for experienced coastal paddlers led by advanced paddlers on days with swell below 4 feet and winds to 15 knots; however, we don't recommend joining multiday tours because conditions can worsen overnight, leaving you stranded on the beach.

Advanced: 19 miles one way from Shelter Cove when combined with previous trip. (8 miles one way from Bear Harbor, or 8 miles round-trip from Usal north to Little Jackass.) Strong coastal skills required: rough-water paddling and rescue skills, water reading, navigation, advanced surf landings in loaded boats through rocks and large surf onto steep beaches. Not recommended in swells above 6–8 feet or winds above 20–25 knots.

TRIP DURATION: Part day, full day, or overnight.

NAVIGATION AIDS: See Route 1: Shelter Cove.

TIDAL INFORMATION: More landings possible on cliff-front beaches at low tide.

CAUTIONS: Standard open-coast cautions (see Route 1: Shelter Cove). Also, if camping overnight on beaches en route, worsening sea conditions could leave you stranded, facing a long, steep hike out without your boat. A weather radio is a must: Unlike most cliffy coastal areas in the state, reception here is good throughout. If the swell is forecast to be over 6 feet, you may want to reconsider.

TRIP PLANNING: Although you could paddle the 19 miles from Shelter Cove to Usal in a long day, we recommend camping, giving yourself two to four days for exploring, layovers, and weather days. Bring extra food in case you get weathered in and have strong paddling skills and lots of experience—then get lucky with the weather. Once you leave the protection of Shelter Cove, beaches are few, and the prevailing winds will be in your face if you try to turn around. You can try to avoid wind by paddling early in the day, but fog could be a problem. Don't forget to pick up the required camping permits from Usal Beach or Needle Rock Visitor Center. This extremely challenging trip has shuttle logistics to match. After dropping the shuttle car at Usal Beach, you have two main options, both of them ugly: continue bumping down unpaved Usal Road (assuming it hasn't washed out again) to Shelter Cove or return to Highway 1, head north to Highway 101 to Garberville and take Shelter Cove Road. Either way you're facing about three hours in the car. (Launching from Shelter Cove instead of Bear Harbor will double the paddling mileage for the same horrendous shuttle.) It's enough to make you consider a third, less-ambitious option: skip the shuttle and paddle north out of Usal and back.

LAUNCH SITE: See Route 1: Shelter Cove for directions to Shelter Cove or Bear Harbor. To get to Usal Beach, take Highway 1 and go 3 miles north of Rockport and turn west on County Road 431, 6 miles of rugged dirt road not recommended for RVs.

DIRECTIONS

START—MILE 11.0 (from Route 1): Continue south from **Bear Harbor Camp** along more thousand-foot cliffs with no landings. *Caution:* Before leaving the road access at Bear Harbor, check your weather radio (and your luck). Landing sites to the south are few, and the beaches are steep and more exposed.

MILE 13.5: A brief break in the cliffs, the beach at the mouth of **Jackass Creek** makes a better landmark than a landing. It's steep and exposed,

Bear Harbor to Usal Beach & Beyond

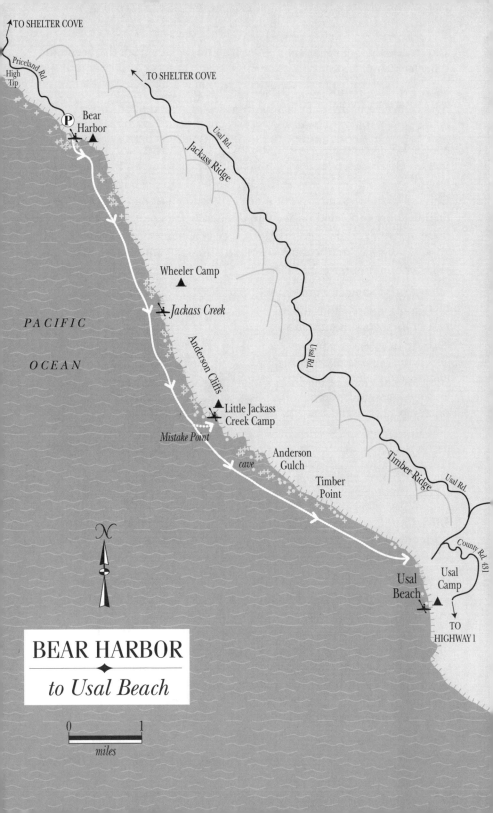

TO SHELTER COVE

Priceland Rd.

High Tip

P

Bear Harbor

TO SHELTER COVE

Usal Rd.

Jackass Ridge

PACIFIC

OCEAN

Wheeler Camp

Jackass Creek

Anderson Cliffs

Little Jackass Creek Camp

Mistake Point

cave

Anderson Gulch

Timber Point

Usal Rd.

Timber Ridge

Usal Rd.

County Rd. 431

Usal Beach

Usal Camp

TO HIGHWAY 1

N

BEAR HARBOR
to Usal Beach

0   1

miles

and the closest campsites are a good half-mile schlep from the beach to **Wheeler Camp**.

MILE 14: Where **Anderson Cliffs** begin, the precipice steepens noticeably (assuming there's no fog) just when you thought the landscape couldn't get any more vertical.

MILE 15.5: Tucked in a cove in the meager lee of **Mistake Point, Little Jackass Creek Camp** has excellent creek-side camping on the beach and an outhouse 0.25 mile up the trail. The hike along the edge of Anderson Cliffs gives an awesome overview of the coastline just paddled. *Caution:* Slightly more protected on the left, the beach's steep dumping shore break resembles the infamous Monastery Beach near Carmel. *Sidetrips:* If conditions are calm, the narrow arch in Mistake Point is runnable but risky, with no room for mistakes.

MILE 17.0: The next 1 mile or so to **Timber Point** is the best of the best—more steep cliffs, sea stacks, tiny coves, and runnable rock gardens, climaxing in a long, narrow, T-shaped cave with three openings near Anderson Gulch. *Caution:* These rock gardens are as challenging as any on the West Coast and more remote than most. This

is no place to take chances or to miss your roll if you capsize.

MILE 19.0: The next break in the cliffs is the roadhead at **Usal Beach**. With only moderate protection from prevailing seas, the beach is at least wide and sandy and not as steep as those before it.

OTHER OPTIONS: The most conservative option is to paddle 4 miles north from Usal Beach to Little Jackass and back as a day trip or overnighter. The next 10 miles south of Usal to Hardy Creek, where Highway 1 rejoins the coast, are not as scenic—the coastal mountans fade back to their usual size and steepness—but the paddling terrain is some of the best. Several miles of incredible sea-stack rock gardens cover the lower half. Unfortunately there are only a few low-tide beaches on the route and no camping possible except at Rockport Bay, which is a private campground for Louisiana-Pacific employees.

Anderson Gulch Cave

The cliffs continue to tower overhead as the five of us round another sharp point. "Cave," someone calls out, but none of us paddles toward it. We only note the western exposure of its small, seaward opening, a narrow throat of jagged rock and crashing surf that foams at the mouth as it swallows a set of four 6-foot waves. "Ain't no place for kayakers," I think. In the lee of the point, however, maybe 100 feet from the mouth, we notice a better-protected side entry from the south, a single-wide garage door leading into darkness and the sloshing guts of midcave. As a set boils through, I paddle closer to gawk, certain the ceiling's too low to be passable. During the ensuing lull, however, I'm drawn toward the cave, a moth to the flame. Paddling backward to facilitate a hasty retreat, I duck through the narrow opening and discover a vaulted ceiling with plenty of head room and steep, deep walls. My favorite cave type: lots of bounce and noise but little danger. I slosh around inside for awhile, tensing up as the next set pours in down the throat, like an avalanche, frothing off the sides and ceiling, cutting off light, only to reach the wider midcave section to reform as a swell that bobs me gently up toward the ceiling, then sloshes off the sides, creating a confusion of chop but also a pillow of safety that keeps my kayak from washing into the black walls. I beckon the others with a raised paddle—"it's not as bad as it looks," I think—but only Billy shares my twisted idea of a good time. We bounce around together through another set, bracing and hooting and laughing in the din. And Billy's had enough. He flees out the side, and I eye the back opening, a narrow slot between rocks, but a short enough sprint to run between waves. Digging hard into black water, the freight train echo of the next wave hard on my heels, I burst out into sunlight, giddy with adrenaline.

Where to Eat & Where to Stay

RESTAURANTS & LODGING   See Route 1: Shelter Cove.
CAMPING   Camping is allowed only in established sites within the park. The required backcountry permits are available at *Usal Beach* or *Needle Rock Visitor Center.* Call (707) 986–7711 for maps and information.

Route 3:

━━ ━━ ━━ ━ ━━ ━━ ━━ ━ ━━ ━━ ━━ ━ ━━ ━━ ━━ ━━ ➤

Russian Gulch to Point Cabrillo & Beyond

Russian Gulch is an excellent alternative for experienced paddlers who've already done the more popular, *and more protected,* Van Damme (see rte. 5 for an introduction to paddling the area's caves), and who are looking for some new caves to explore. Limited options for less-experienced paddlers also exist.

TRIP HIGHLIGHTS: World-class sea caves and rock gardens, seabirds, seals, and solitude.

TRIP RATING:

Beginner: Although the launch site is accessible to beginners on calm days, there is only a half mile of protection before the open ocean. It's strongly recommended that you stay close to the beach and well away from rocks and caves unless you have expert guid-ance, in which case you might be able to access the first set of coves and caves a half mile north in seas below 3 feet and wind to 15 knots.

Intermediate: 1–4 miles for those with previous coastal paddling experience and good sea sense in swells below 4 feet and winds to 15 knots; the guidance of an experienced cave paddler is highly recommended.

Advanced: 5+ miles of rock garden heaven await experienced paddlers with strong open-coast skills. Seas above 6 feet limit access to most caves and rock gardens.

TRIP DURATION: Part to full day.

NAVIGATION AIDS: USGS: Mendocino (7.5 minute) and NOAA chart 18628. Wx radio: "Cape Mendocino to Point Arena"; buoys: Point Arena.

TIDAL INFORMATION: Lower tides give better protection from outer reefs, more beach access, and more headroom in caves.

CAUTIONS: Waves, submerged rocks, clapotis, wind, and fog.

TRIP PLANNING: Best protection with lower tide and swell. Although it's possible to paddle outside the reef in swells of 8 feet or more, that's missing the point: To access the caves and rock gardens inside the reef, the calmer the better (only experts recommended in swells above 6 feet). Paddle north early in the day and return with the wind. Be very careful and skilled.

LAUNCH SITE: Two miles north of Mendocino on Highway 1: Head west into **Russian Gulch State Park**, turn left, and follow signs to the beach. There is a $5.00 day use fee; rest rooms, and cold outdoor showers available. **Alternate launch site:** Caspar Anchorage 3 miles north. Head west through Caspar and wind your way down to the beach.

START: Contour along the cliffs to the north, exploring a few small caves and arches before leaving the protection of the gulch. *Caution:* The dangers of submerged rocks, waves, and caves persist along this entire route.

MILE 0.25: Exposure increases immediately as you round the point and head north. *Sidetrips:* On a calm day, less-experienced paddlers can access the small, secluded beach inside the southern arm of the cove for some solitude.

MILE 0.5: Work your way inside the reef, if possible, into a **complex of coves** that feature some of the area's finest caves, arches, chutes, and rock gardens, as well as several small, hidden beaches. *Caution:* Watch for seal haul outs.

MILE 1.0: As you round the next **minor point** (where the Point Cabrillo Lighthouse comes into view), exposure increases, so either cut back inside the reef for more excellent coves, caves, beaches, and rock gardens for the next mile or so or turn around if it's too rough. *Caution:* The farther north you paddle up this coast, the more exposed it becomes.

MILE 2.25: **Point Cabrillo** makes a good spot to turn around as conditions get even rougher beyond. *Sidetrip:* If not too rough, continue to some remote beaches just below Caspar Anchorage or go all the way to the beach at Caspar.

OTHER OPTIONS: Run a shuttle and do a one-way trip from Caspar down to Russian Gulch or from Russian Gulch down to Mendocino or Van Damme.

Where to Eat & Where to Stay

RESTAURANTS, LODGING, & CAMPING See Route 4: Big River for information about restaurants, lodging, and camping.

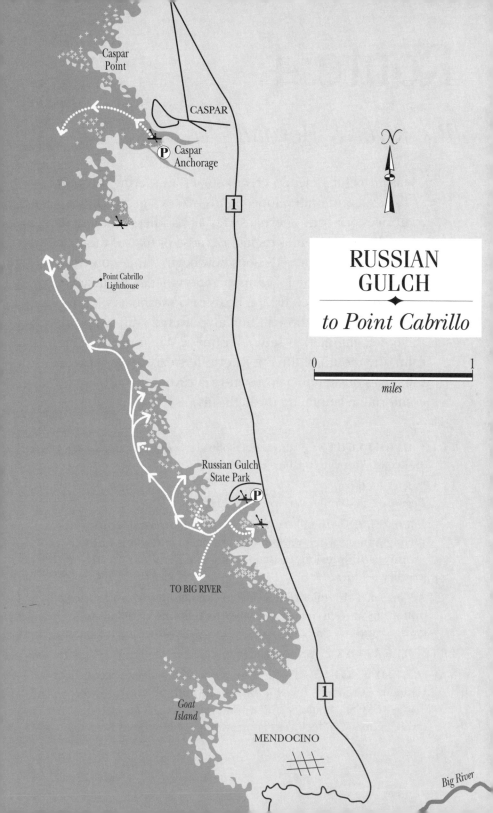

Caspar
Point

CASPAR

P Caspar
Anchorage

1

Point Cabrillo
Lighthouse

RUSSIAN
GULCH

◆

to Point Cabrillo

0   1

miles

Russian Gulch
State Park

P

TO BIG RIVER

1

*Goat
Island*

MENDOCINO

Big River

Route 4:

━ ━ ━ ━ ━ ━ ━ ━ ━ ━ ━ ━ ━ ━ ━ ➤

Big River & Beyond

This peaceful, emerald green estuary wandering through forested and undeveloped lands makes a great trip for novices or a sane alternative for all paddlers on those days when the sea beyond is raging. Because of turn-of-the-century logging, the redwoods now begin 2 miles upstream and remnants of the logging operations act as landmarks along the banks. Few fishing boats or powerboats venture here, leaving only those in human-powered craft to absorb the quiet, engulfed by serene lushness. When the ocean is calm, the mouth of the Big River offers excellent access to the area's outstanding coves and sea caves for those comfortable launching through surf.

TRIP HIGHLIGHTS: Calm water, solitude, redwoods; access to surf and coastal touring with excellent caves.

TRIP RATING:

Beginner: 1–16 miles very protected estuary.

Intermediate: 1–16 miles with access to open-coast sidetrips and surfing options when waves are below 3 feet and winds to 15 knots for those with previous coastal touring experience or an advanced paddler leading.

Advanced: 1–16 miles with access to coastal sidetrips and surfing options in waves to 6 feet and winds to 25 knots; excellent rock gardens and sea caves.

TRIP DURATION: Part to full day.

NAVIGATION AIDS: Big River map is available from Catch a Canoe boat rentals (707–937–0273) on south side of Big River bridge. USGS: *Mendocino* (7.5 minute) and NOAA chart 18628. Wx radio: "Cape Mendocino to Point Arena"; buoys: Point Arena.

TIDAL INFORMATION: The river is tidally influenced for 8 miles. (We've seen a harbor seal 4 miles upstream.)

CAUTIONS: Strong ocean-going currents under Highway 1 bridge at the river mouth during ebb tide. Near the launch site, afternoon winds blowing upriver are common during summer. Potential for flooding during winter.

TRIP PLANNING: Ride the flood tide on your way in and the ebb on your way out for an easier time. Save some energy to fight the upriver winds on the last mile or so of the return.

LAUNCH SITE: Immediately north of the Big River bridge on Highway 1 turn away from the ocean onto North Big River Road, leading to the broad dirt pull out on the flood plain under the bridge, which offers easy access to the river. The easiest launch is at the farthest beach from the bridge, but it sometimes gets crowded; small trails through the grass make possible other launch sites along this large parking area. No fees or facilities.

DIRECTIONS

START: Head east, winding upriver. Conifers and rhododendrons line the banks. *Caution:* During a falling tide, potentially hazardous currents sweep seaward into the surf. *Sidetrips:* On calm days, surf-savvy paddlers can play in the waves or explore the cliffs and caves in Mendocino Bay (see Other Options).

MILE 2.0: Large pilings and small landing beaches on either side of the river mark **New Boom,** remnants of a dam that gathered logs to be floated downriver to mill. Beyond here the alder and willow woodlands give way to redwoods, and the river becomes more narrow and convoluted.

MILE 3.0: Short pilings, the remains of logging train tracks parallel the left bank.

MILE 3.5: Just beyond the **large landslide** on the right bank is a sandy beach with a grassy area that can be a nice place to take a break, but it can be a bit of a steep scramble for 5 or 6 feet. *Sidetrip:* Continue on through more beautiful forest another mile or so to **Oxbow Marsh** until eventually the kayaking will be restricted by lack of water, approximately 6–8 miles from the mouth, depending on the tide height.

Big River & Beyond

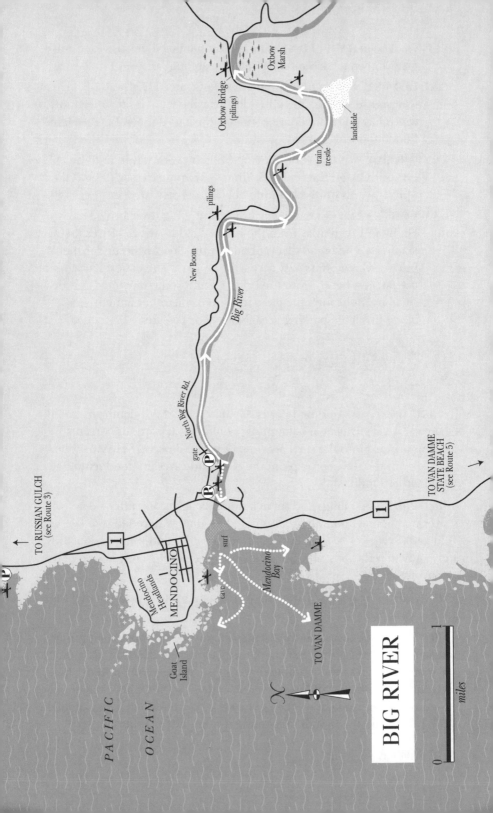

BIG RIVER

PACIFIC

OCEAN

TO RUSSIAN GULCH
(see Route 3)

Mendocino
Headlands

MENDOCINO

Goat
Island

caves

surf

Mendocino
Bay

TO VAN DAMME

gate

North Big River Rd.

New Boom

Big River

pilings

train
trestle

Oxbow Bridge
(pilings)

Oxbow
Marsh

landslide

TO VAN DAMME
STATE BEACH
(see Route 5)

miles

0   1

MILE 7.0: The final 1 mile of the return to the launch site can be against the coastal winds that funnel into the mouth of the river and under the bridge. Use the banks as windbreaks when possible.

OTHER OPTIONS: On calm days, intermediates can launch through small surf and explore up to a mile in the protection of the cliffs on the north side of Mendocino Bay, paddling around sea stacks and into some of the area's best caves to find isolated beaches beneath the bluffs. Experienced open-coast kayakers can leave the bay and explore the rock gardens up to Goat Island and beyond. Or they can do one-way coastal tours down to Van Damme or down from Russian Gulch.

Plan B: Big River Paddlers' Refuge

Plan A that weekend was to paddle Mendocino's famous sea caves, but the sea had other ideas: Saturday morning the weather radio was calling for a gale warning with winds in excess of 35 knots and swells to 15 feet. As we stood on the bluffs overlooking Mendocino Bay watching waves slam against cliffs in huge explosions of spray the sea needed no sign to announce Area Closed: Cave Making in Progress. Time for Plan B. The best laid paddling plans, we tell our students, have fall-back options and we often slide well into the alphabet in our quest for safety and fun. In a Mendocino gale, Plan B stands for Big River. Within 1 mile or so of the river's mouth, the ocean's roar muted as the river narrowed, and we meandered into second growth redwood forest. On either side the towering wall of woods provided an eerie calm. After we stopped for lunch on a small beach, a light mist began to fall, further deepening the stillness. We pulled up the hoods of our anoraks, snug and warm despite the weather, and floated silently through the forest's embrace.

Where to Eat & Where to Stay

RESTAURANTS There are many fine selections in town, as a quick preview: **Mendocino Cafe** (707–937–2422) serves tasty Pacific Rim fare, **Mendocino Market** (707–937–3474) makes deluxe deli sandwiches for lunch. **Mendo Juice Joint** (707–937–4033) could supply the morning charge of espresso or smoothie starting at 6:30 A.M. **Bayview Cafe** (707–937–4197) has tasty shrimp tostadas, fish and chips, and other affordable delights for lunch or dinner. **LODGING** In addition to lodging, **Sweetwater Gardens** (800–300–4140 or 707–937–4140) has hot tubs, saunas, and massages available whether or not you are staying there. The **MacCallum House Inn and Restaurant** offers Victorian-style lodging and fine cuisine (800–609–0492) and is also right in the village. For many other choices contact the Chamber of Commerce (707–961–6300). **CAMPING** **Van Damme State Park,** in the pine forest just south of Mendocino, and **Russian Gulch State Park** just north, have tent sites, hot showers, and hook-ups. Make reservations through Park Net (800–444–7275). **Mendocino Campground** has showers, fish cleaning station, and lots of trees among its sites (707–937–3130). (See Route 6: Albion for more campgrounds.)

Big River & Beyond

Route 5:
-- -- -- -- -- -- -- -- -- -- -- -- -- ➤

Van Damme State Beach

Although the craggy Mendocino coast is among the more scenic shorelines in a state famous for its beautiful shores, what puts Mendo on the map as one of the planet's premier paddling destinations is the number and complexity of its sea caves. Many are short and straight, little more than arches, while others tunnel 100 yards from one hidden cove to the next. A few caves are big and simple as barns, still others snake and divide into multiple passages so dark we use waterproof head lamps to find our way to the back. The easiest and safest place to get into a sea cave here is probably from Van Damme State Beach. Its sandy, south-facing launch beach together with its nearby parking lot all make it the region's most accessible and protected sea-caving area. In addition to its caves, there is an excellent variety of marine life—from seabirds and seals to a rich intertidal zone.

TRIP HIGHLIGHTS: World-class sea caves and rock gardens, seabirds, seals, and excellent tide pools.

TRIP RATING:

Beginner: 1–3 miles is possible on days with swells below 4 feet and winds below 10 knots, but it is strongly recommended that you stay away from rocks and caves without expert guidance (Lost Coast Kayaking (707–937–2434) runs half-day tours on sit-on-tops from Van Damme). Helmets recommended for paddling anywhere near rocks.

Intermediate: 1–5 miles for those with previous coastal paddling experience and good sea sense on days with swells below 4 feet and winds below 15 knots; the guidance of an experienced cave paddler is recommended, especially beyond the protection of the cove at Van Damme.

Advanced: 7+ miles of rock garden heaven await experienced paddlers with strong open-coast skills. Seas above 6 feet limit access to most caves and rock gardens.

TRIP DURATION: Part to full day.

NAVIGATION AIDS: USGS: *Mendocino and Albion* (7.5 minute) and NOAA chart 18628. Wx radio: "Cape Mendocino to Point Arena"; buoys: Point Arena.

TIDAL INFORMATION: Lower tides give better protection from outer reefs, more beach access, and more headroom in caves.

CAUTIONS: Waves, submerged rocks, clapotis, wind, and fog.

TRIP PLANNING: Best protection is with lower tide and swell. Altogether it's possible to paddle outside the reef in swells of 8 feet or more, that's missing the point: to access the caves and rock gardens inside the reef, the calmer the better (only experts recommended in swells above 6 feet). Paddle north early in the day and return with the wind. Be very careful and skilled.

LAUNCH SITE: Van Damme State Beach is located on Highway 1, 2 miles south of Mendocino. Free parking, outhouse, and cold outdoor showers.

DIRECTIONS

START: Launch from **Van Damme State Beach,** contouring along the cliffs to the north past rock gardens and a couple of nice caves. *Caution:* The dangers of submerged rocks and waves persist along this entire route.

MILE 0.5: At the west end of the cove, it is possible *on calm days* to turn north up the coast for another 0.5 mile and explore mazelike channels, caves, and hidden coves of the **"inside passage,"** a semiprotected route between the offshore rocks and the cliffs. *Caution:* On rough days it's better to turn around and skip the inside passage, which becomes increasingly more exposed to the north.

MILE 1.0: At the **end of the inside passage,** the channel gradually narrows to naught; either turn around and retrace your route, or, if the

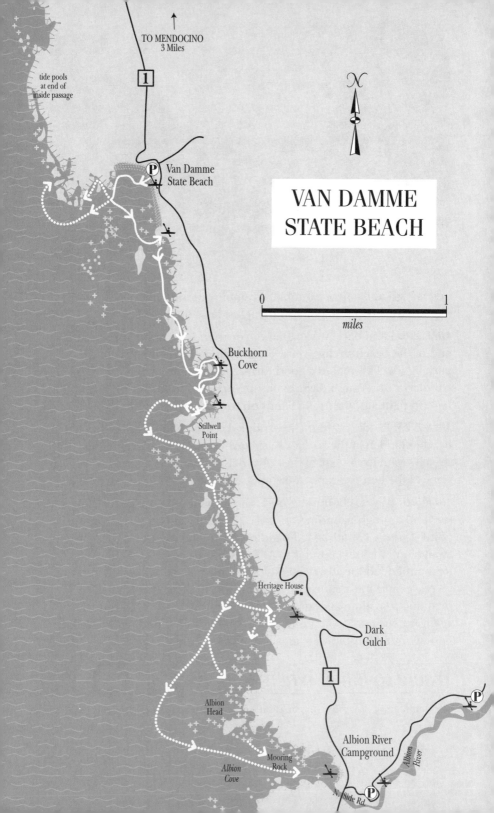

TO MENDOCINO
3 Miles

1

tide pools
at end of
inside passage

N

P Van Damme
State Beach

VAN DAMME
STATE BEACH

0   1

miles

Buckhorn
Cove

Stillwell
Point

Heritage House

Dark
Gulch

1

Albion
Head

P

Albion River
Campground

*Albion
River*

*Albion
Cove*

Mooring
Rock

N. Side Rd

P

tide is high and you are nimble, scramble out onto the rocks and explore the **great tide pool** on the left side of the passage.

MILE 2.0: Land back at Van Damme or round the point at the south end of the beach to discover a small, **secluded cove** away from the parking lot. This makes a good turn-around point for less-experienced paddlers or on rough days. Exposure increases to the south, and you'll have to fight any afternoon winds on your return.

MILE 2.75: Paddle down the cave-riddled coastline to find small, secluded beaches hidden in the back of **Buckhorn Cove.** When it's calm, this stretch—with its maze of arches, channels, chutes, and sea stacks—provides some of the best paddling in the area. *Caution:* Watch for seal haul outs.

MILE 3.0: Waves rebounding off **Stillwell Point** often make for confused seas and a rough rounding, so this is generally a good turn-around point. *Sidetrip:* For advanced paddlers more fine caves and rock gardens await along the next 3 miles to **Albion Cove** (see rte. 6). *Caution:* Recommended for advanced paddlers only beyond Stillwell: Exposure increases and the assumption is that if you've come this far, you're planning to paddle all the way to Albion rather than try to return against the wind. If you are not very comfortable rounding Stillwell, don't continue; Albion Head is usually much worse.

Where to Eat & Where to Stay

See Route 4: Big River for information on restaurants, lodging, and camping.

Van Damme State Beach

Paddling in Caves:
Thrills, Threats, Tips, & Terms

A hundred feet into the cave's deepening shadows, our kayaks bob on half-lit, stained-glass seas. Switching on our head lamps, we paddle around a corner into darkness, the cave twisting and turning like the inside of a giant seashell. Our lights reveal a narrowing fissure, its walls glossed with coralline algae that glistens conch-pink below the barnacles where the tide has fallen. Since before Odysseus stumbled bewitched into Circe's lair, the damp musk of an unexplored sea cave has cast an irresistible lure. But you have to be careful. Sea caves are one of the great thrills and greatest dangers of ocean kayaking. Although Mendo's caves are sometimes quite calm, any swells entering can become compressed laterally and surge toward the ceiling. This can be exciting if there is enough headroom and paddling skill, or it can be dangerous. In the book, *Deep Trouble*, a compilation of accident reports from *Sea Kayaker* magazine, one paddler reported serious spine injury when a large wave bounced his head off the ceiling. Consider the waves that carved the caves and stay out when there's "cave making in progress." Before entering any cave, no matter how calm it looks, watch for several minutes to see how rough the waves are inside during large sets. If you don't have a reliable Eskimo roll, consider how difficult it will be to perform a rescue in a dark, sloshing cave. We sometimes paddle backward into caves to facilitate a hasty retreat. Caves with two openings are safer to run when facing the direction of the swell, if possible, to decrease the chance of surfing out of control into the rocks. But our best tip would be this: *Don't try to learn how to paddle in caves by reading a book*. Find a knowledgeable professional and take lessons, then gain experience with skilled paddlers around. Know your limits, and respect the ocean's power. Here's some caving lingo, in case you were curious: a *cave* that passes through a piece of land and comes out the other side is, technically speaking, a *tunnel*, unless of course it's higher than it is long, then it's an *arch*. We've used the term *cave* loosely in the book to describe all three.

Route 6:

■ ■ ■ ■ ■ ■ ■ ■ ■ ■ ■ ■ ■ ➤

Albion to Dark Gulch & Beyond

For novice and intermediate paddlers, the narrow gorge of Albion Cove, with its dramatic and scenic cliffs, offers even better protection than the more popular Van Damme (see rte. 5); unfortunately, there are no sea caves until you leave this protection and round Albion Head. Advanced paddlers will find this rugged stretch to the north riddled with some of Mendo's best caves and rock gardens—and most challenging conditions—while less-experienced paddlers can enjoy the shelter of the cove or explore several miles upriver along the quiet, tree-lined banks of the Albion River.

TRIP HIGHLIGHTS: Access to both quiet water and world-class sea caves and rock gardens.

TRIP RATING:

Beginner: 4-mile flat-water trip up river, or 1 mile of good protection on calm days to Albion Head, where the ocean gets rough in a hurry. It's strongly recommended that you don't paddle past Mooring Rock without expert guidance.

Intermediate: 1–4 miles for those with previous coastal paddling experience and good sea sense in swells below 4 feet and winds to 15 knots; not recommended beyond Albion Head without advanced paddler leading.

Advanced: 5+ miles of rock garden heaven await experienced paddlers with strong open-coast skills. Seas above 6 feet limit access to most caves and rock gardens.

TRIP DURATION: Part to full day.

NAVIGATION AIDS: USGS: *Albion* (7.5 minute) and NOAA chart 18628. Wx radio: "Cape Mendocino to Point Arena"; buoys: Point Arena.

TIDAL INFORMATION: Lower tides give better protection from outer reefs, more beach access, and more headroom in caves.

CAUTIONS: Waves, submerged rocks, clapotis, wind, and fog.

TRIP PLANNING: Best protection with lower tide and swell. Although it's possible to paddle outside the reef in swells of 8 feet or more, that's missing the point: To access the caves and rock gardens inside the reef, the calmer the sea the better are your chances (only experts recommended in swells above 6 feet). Paddle north early in the day and return with the wind. Be very careful and skilled beyond Albion Head. If you're planning to land at Dark Gulch, scout conditions beforehand from the overlook at Heritage House.

LAUNCH SITE: To reach the launch ramp at Albion River Campground from Highway 1, turn east on North Side Road, just north of the Albion River bridge and follow it down to the water. There is a $5.00 launch fee per kayak. Restrooms available. **Alternate launch site:** Schooners Landing, 0.5 mile farther on North Side Road. The charge here is $10.00 per vehicle to launch. Rest rooms available.

DIRECTIONS

START: Paddle west down river past the boat docks. *Caution:* Stay out of the way of fishing boats in this narrow channel. *Sidetrip:* Wind up to 4 miles upriver with a rising tide, sit-on-top kayaks available to rent for this trip through Dive Crazy Adventures (707–937–3079) in the Schooners Landing campground.

MILE 0.25: Leaving the **mouth of the Albion River,** contour along the steep cliffs to the north, passing the wide sandy beach at the river mouth. *Caution:* The dangers of submerged rocks, waves, and caves persist along this entire route.

MILE 0.5: Navigational marker atop **Mooring Rock** at the end of the "inner cove" is a good place for beginners to turn around if not accompanied by an advanced paddler. Beyond this point are a couple small beaches in hidden coves on the right that can be landable if swell and tide are down. *Caution:* When seas are up, the outer cove can get quite rough.

Albion to Dark Gulch & Beyond

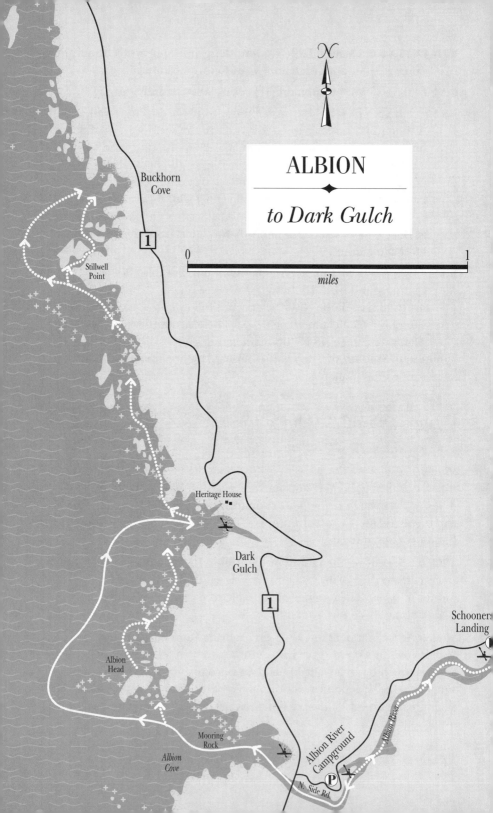

ALBION

to Dark Gulch

Buckhorn
Cove

[1]

Stillwell
Point

0   1
miles

Heritage House

Dark
Gulch

[1]

Albion
Head

Schooners
Landing

Mooring
Rock

*Albion
Cove*

Albion River
Campground

Albion River

P

N. Side Rd.

MILE 1.0: **Albion Head** (a large sea stack that only appears to be an attached headland) is a good place to reassess conditions or turn around. *Caution:* Advanced coastal touring skills are required beyond Albion Head. It can be one of the roughest roundings in this area, and it will only get rougher as wind and seas rise during the day. Swing wide to round the rocks that extend well out to sea off the point. *Sidetrip:* On calm days skilled paddlers can try running the shortcut gap between Albion Head and shore, but it is long and rocky and can be quite dangerous if waves are breaking through it.

MILE 1.5: Good caves and rock gardens along this exposed stretch to the sandy, well-protected beach at **Dark Gulch.** *Caution:* When the swell is up, waves breaking on submerged rocks at the entrance to the cove can make getting into the cove difficult to dangerous. *Sidetrip:* Continue north past more caves and sea stacks for another 1.5 miles to the fine landing beaches in **Buckhorn Cove** (see rte. 5).

OTHER OPTIONS: Run a shuttle and do a one-way trip south from Van Damme (see rte. 5) or head down the very exposed cliffs south of Albion to the mouth of the Navarro River. Options abound in this area for advanced paddlers.

Where to Eat & Where to Stay

R E S T A U R A N T S The **Albion River Inn** (800–479–7944) across from the turn off on Highway 1 features fresh local seafood, outstanding views, and fine wines, but you'll definitely want to shower and change into nice clothes first. There are more options in Mendocino 6 miles north. (See also Route 4: Big River.) **L O D G I N G** Perched on the cliffs overlooking the cove, **Albion River Inn** (800–479–7944) has rooms with ocean view, fireplace, and spa. (Also see Route 4: Big River.) **C A M P I N G** Although quite conveniently located at the put in, the sites at **Albion River Campground** (707–937–0606) and **Schooners Landing** (707–937–5707) are more crowded and less attractive than others in the area. (See also Route 4: Big River.)

Point Reyes National Seashore & Vicinity

Route 7:

━━ ━━ ━━ ━━ ━━ ━━ ━━ ━━ ━━ ━━ ➤

Russian River

Winding past hills covered in coastal scrub at the mouth, this peaceful ribbon of water meanders through willow thickets and dense evergreen stands as you continue inland. The relative solitude, scenery, and wildlife along this stretch make it an excellent place for an easy day trip, despite the proximity of Highway 116, which runs the length of the river. A variety of birds—from cormorants and ducks to shorebirds and osprey—are commonly seen along with harbor seal and the occasional river otter. Upriver, currents are generally easy to paddle against and helpful when returning against the afternoon winds. Kayak camping is available at a hike-in environmental camp near the put in, as well as at two drive-in private campgrounds further upstream. Although camping here is easily accessible to beginners, it is not very isolated. For more skilled and adventurous paddlers seeking solitude, the coastline beyond the river mouth is much more remote— thick with cliffs, rock gardens, sea stacks, and surf.

TRIP HIGHLIGHTS: Excellent protection, wildlife, warm(er) water to practice rescue skills, with easy access to kayak camping possibilities and coastal touring.

TRIP RATING:

Beginner: 1–20+ miles of well-protected water.

Intermediate: 1–20+ miles with access to coastal touring in waves to 3 feet and winds to 15 knots.

Advanced: 24+ miles, with access to coastal rock gardens and surf.

TRIP DURATION: Part day, full day, or overnight(s).

NAVIGATION AIDS: USGS: *Duncans Mills* (7.5 minute). Wx radio: "Point Arena to Pigeon Point"; buoys: Bodega Bay, Point Reyes.

TIDAL INFORMATION: Currents at mouth but little effect on water levels.

CAUTIONS: At river mouth, avoid seal haul outs, ocean-going currents, and strong afternoon winds.

TRIP PLANNING: Calmest conditions exist generally early in the morning or evening. Expect strong afternoon wind blowing upriver within a few miles of the mouth, so paddle early to avoid returning against it or save some energy. Although downstream current is generally weak (except during storm runoff), you might make better progress upriver by staying near the banks and out of the main flow. Securing a good campsite at Willow Creek Environmental Camp can take some doing, especially on busy weekends. There are only ten first-come, first-serve sites, not all of which have direct river access. We suggest driving to Willow Creek to pick a site before you paddle, so you'll be sure to have one when you arrive by boat.

LAUNCH SITE: Sonoma Coast State Beach Visitor Center in Jenner on Highway 1 is just past the more prominent Sea Gull Gifts and Deli, which is the first building on the left as you enter town from the south. Outhouses, boat ramp, and parking; no fee. **Alternate launch sites:** Bridgehaven Campground lies on the ocean side of the Highway 1 bridge on the south bank. Willow Creek Environmental Camp is 1.5 miles upriver from the bridge, also on the south bank. Head east on Willow Creek Road (next to Tandoor restaurant across from the Bridgehaven Campground driveway) and turn left when you see the sign to the campground.

DIRECTIONS

START: Head downstream from the visitor center to circumnavigate **Penny Island;** some landings are possible, but much of the island is muddy or overgrown. *Sidetrip:* Paddle right along the sand spit to see the seals near the mouth; land near pilings to portage to **Goat Rock Beach** (instead of paddling past seals) to launch through surf and access rock gardens. *Caution:* Be alert for seals, ocean-going currents, and surf.

MILE 2.5: **Highway 1 Bridge** and small beach on right at **Bridgehaven Campground.**

MILE 3.0: Extensive **gravel bar.** *Caution:* Avoid shallow water on the right and harbor seals resting on logs along the left bank.

MILE 3.5: **Willow Creek Environmental Camp** is hidden in the willow thicket behind the long, sand- and-gravel beach on the right, across from a prominent gray highway road cut. The two sites with the best river access are 50 yards upriver from the long beach and up a steep bank from a small beach. There is room for maybe five or six boats.

OTHER OPTIONS: The Russian River is navigable for 30 miles or so from Healdsburg on down with most of the river towns (Duncans Mills, Monte Rio, Guerneville, etc.) en route having parks with launch access and private campgrounds. Development increases farther inland, however: Homes along the river become prevalent, along with swimmers, inner tubers, and people in general.

Where to Eat & Where to Stay

RESTAURANT   **Sea Gull Gifts and Deli** (707–865–2594) has fine sandwiches and the **Sizzling Tandoor** (707–865–0625) specializes in Indian cuisine. **LODGING**   **Jenner Inn & Cottages** (707–865–2377) and the **River's End Resort** (707–865–2484) overlook the bluffs of Jenner. (See also Route 8: Bodega Harbor.) **CAMPING**   **Bridgehaven** has campsites with showers for $20; (707–865–2473). Primitive campsites with outhouses, tables, and fire pits at **Willow Creek Environmental Camp** for $10, first-come, first serve.

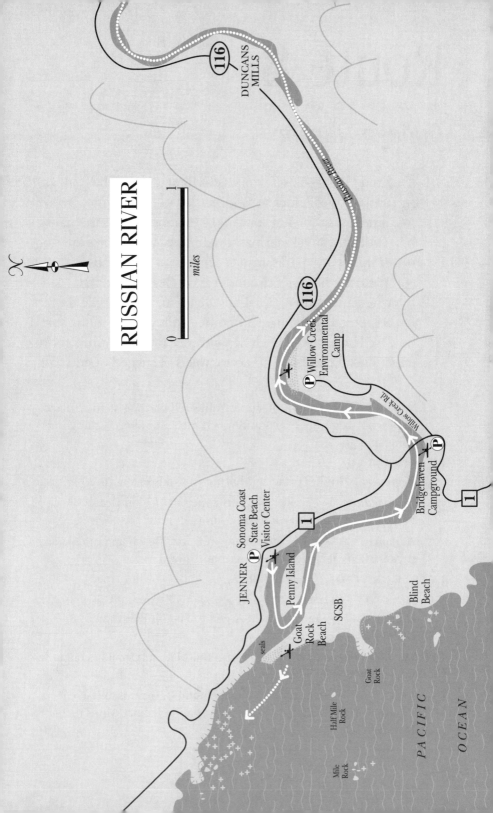

RUSSIAN RIVER

miles

0

116

DUNCANS MILLS

Russian River

116

Willow Creek Environmental Camp

Willow Creek Rd.

Bridgehaven Campground

1

1

JENNER

Sonoma Coast State Beach Visitor Center

Penny Island

seals

Goat Rock Beach

SCSB

Blind Beach

Goat Rock

Half Mile Rock

Mile Rock

PACIFIC

OCEAN

Route 8:

Bodega Harbor

lfred Hitchcock's *The Birds* was filmed in nearby Bodega, and birds still flock to Bodega Bay to feed on the rich mudflats in the harbor. A boat channel bisects the harbor's tideflats; small marinas, restaurants, and homes line the north shore; and parks, dunes, and grassy headlands complete the harbor's circumference. Beginners and intermediates can enjoy a 4-mile flat-water loop inside the harbor, practice reentries and other skills, or play in the surf on a well-protected stretch of sandy ocean beach, while more experienced paddlers can access miles of rugged open coast.

TRIP HIGHLIGHTS: Protection from swell, birding, a good place to practice beginning skills and watch the commercial fishing fleet come and go.

TRIP RATING:

Beginner: 1–4 miles protected harbor in winds below 10–15 knots.

Intermediate: 1–4+ miles with surf zone practice on Doran Beach in waves to 3 feet, and wind to 15 knots.

Advanced: 1–4+ miles with surfing at Doran Beach and open-coast rock gardens at Bodega Head and northward.

TRIP DURATION: Part to full day.

NAVIGATION AIDS: USGS: *Bodega Head* (7.5 minute) and NOAA chart 18643. Wx radio: "Point Arena to Pigeon Point"; buoys: Bodega Bay.

TIDAL INFORMATION: Extensive mudflats and shallows begin to uncover at tide heights below 3 feet.

CAUTIONS: Mudflats, traffic in boat channel, currents at harbor mouth during ebb tide, and fog; waves and offshore winds on Doran Beach.

TRIP PLANNING: Make a clockwise loop, heading north into the harbor before the wind kicks up (leave an hour or two before high tide to ride the incoming current) and have the wind at your back on the return. Although it's possible to paddle here at any tide height if you stay in the boat channel, 3 feet or more of tide is necessary to cross the mudflats at the end of the channel and complete the loop. On a falling tide, you might try crossing the mudflats first and riding the ebb current in the boat channel in a counterclockwise loop. When camping at Doran County Park, choose a campsite that you can both camp at and launch from.

LAUNCH SITE: To reach the boat ramp at Doran County Park from Highway 1, take Doran Park Road just south of the town of Bodega Bay and head west out the sandspit; pass the Doran Beach day-use parking and the campgrounds and look for the boat ramp on the right after you pass the Coast Guard dock. Launch from the beach to left of ramp to avoid traffic. There is a $3.00 parking fee; rest rooms are available. Alternate launch sites: Westside County Park boat ramp costs $3.00, but there are several other free launch sites possible from pull outs along West Shore Road, as well as from Porto Bodega Fishermans'(sic) Marina or at Campbell Cove.

DIRECTIONS

START: Head north from **Doran County Park** boat ramp, skirting the well-marked boat channel to stay out of traffic. *Caution:* Stay out of the posted "Ecological Research Area" adjacent Gaffney Point. *Sidetrip:* Experienced paddlers may head left out the mouth of the harbor (see Other Options).

MILE 0.75: A well-marked side channel leads to the landing beach, campground, and alternative launch site at **Westside County Park.**

MILE 1.0: Spud Point Marina has a small beach where the breakwater meets the shore at the Bosco Keene Promenade. *Caution:* Commercial fishing boat traffic at the mouth of marina. *Sidetrip:* Circumnavigate the inner periphery of the marina except at extreme high or low tides when passage beneath gangplanks may not be possible.

MILE 2.0: Beach and launch ramp at **Porto Bodega** marina.

MILE 2.75: Tides Wharf, the large, white, new-looking building along

Bodega Harbor

the water, has a dingy dock you can land on to stop for lunch at their snack bar, which has outdoor tables and sells fish and chips and sandwiches.

MILE 3.0: Channel Marker #52 marks the end of the boat channel and the beginning of the mudflats. With 3 feet of tide or more, you can cross the mudflats and skirt the salt marsh for some of the harbor's better birding. If the mudflats are exposed, retrace your path along the boat channel.

MILE 4.0: Pass camping area and return to launch site.

OTHER OPTIONS: On calm days intermediates may paddle out the harbor mouth and land through small surf along Doran Beach. *Caution: Scout the beach from shore first* and be careful of currents at the harbor mouth during ebb tide and offshore winds off Doran Beach that can push you out to sea. Two launch sites on Doran Beach, at the north jetty and the day-use parking area, give more direct access to 2 miles of sandy ocean beach. This semisheltered, south-facing beach generally has small surf that gets gradually larger as you head east, making it a good place for surf zone practice and an introductory coastal tour, provided you stay close to shore and the offshore winds don't kick up. Advanced ocean kayakers can head north along the cliffs of Bodega Head or run a shuttle to Dillon Beach or Nicks Cove (see Route 10: North Tomales) and paddle south across 7 miles of open ocean to Tomales Bay. Scout the waves at Dillon Beach from shore before attempting this very advanced crossing.

Where to Eat & Where to Stay

RESTAURANTS   There are many choices along the waterfront in Bodega Bay, especially for seafood, including **Lucas Wharf Restaurant & Bar** (707–875–3522), for finer dining, or **The Dog House** (707–875–2441) and **3 Daughters Deli** (707–875–9408) for food without the frills.   **LODGING**   Bay views are available at the **Bodega Bay Lodge** (800–368–2468, ext. 5; at the corner of Bodega Highway and Doran Park Road) or **The Inn at the Tides** (800–541–7788; across from the Tides Wharf). Or call the chamber of commerce (707–875–3422) for many other choices.   **CAMPING**   Campsites with hot showers are available at **Doran County Park** or **Westside County Park** at a cost of $15 on a first-come basis, but you may need to arrive Friday morning to secure a spot on summer weekends. RV parking is available at **Porto Bodega Fishermans'** (sic) **Marina** (707–875–2354). **Bodega Dunes State Park**, 4 miles north, reserves sites through Park Net (800–444–7275). (See also Tomales Bay area routes.)

PACIFIC

OCEAN

West Shore Rd. / Bay Flat Rd.

P Porto
Bodega

BODEGA BAY

Light

Light

Spud Point Marina P

P *Westside
County Park*
Boat Ramp

▲

*Bodega
Harbor*

Tides
Wharf

52

Mussel
Point

*Horseshoe
Cove*

Gaffney
Point

Closed Research
Area

▲

Boat
Ramp

Doran County Park

salt
marsh

1

Doran Rd.

P Day Use

Doran Beach (surf practice)

P

▲

P

North Jetty

South Jetty
Light

*Bodega
Bay*

N

P Campbell
Cove

Bodega
Head

Light

Bodega Rock

BODEGA HARBOR

0   1

miles

TO DILLON BEACH
6 MILES

Route 9:

Estero Americano

From its humble beginnings in a cow pasture (some local paddlers refer to the launch site as "the muddy ditch"), Estero Americano winds 6 miles to the sea, the scenery improving constantly with each turn downstream. Within a mile of the Holsteins at the put in, the narrow channel slips between grassy, golden hills and widens into salt marsh. In addition to ducks and shorebirds, this riparian corridor is an excellent place to view raptors, including peregrine falcons, golden eagles, and a variety of hawks, soaring over the ridge tops. Near the ocean, the hills become steeper and wilder still, now cloaked in coastal scrub and traversed by deer and elk. When the estero exits a gap in the steep ocean cliffs, the vista is about as far from a cow pasture as you can get. Beyond the cliffs and sea stacks stretches the entire sweep of Bodega Bay, from Bodega Head in the north to Tomales Point in the south; on clear days you can even see Point Reyes headland, 20 miles in the distance. You can hunker out of the wind behind the low dunes at the mouth for lunch, and even camp overnight, if you don't mind sharing the view with a house high on the bluff.

TRIP HIGHLIGHTS: Flatwater, solitude, and wildlife: raptors, elk, and deer.

TRIP RATING:

Beginner: 5–11 miles of flatwater to ocean and back for energetic beginners.

Intermediate: 11 miles round-trip to ocean. Surf practice is possible on very calm days with waves to 3 feet, and winds to 15 knots.

Advanced: 11 miles round-trip to ocean with rock gardens, coastal touring, and difficult surf (with waves above 6 feet and winds above 20 knots).

TRIP DURATION: Part day, full day, or overnight.

NAVIGATION AIDS: USGS *Valley Ford* (7.5 minute), tide book, Wx radio: "Point Arena to Pigeon Point"; buoys: Bodega Bay.

TIDAL INFORMATION: Check tides when the mouth is open to the sea—to get past the shallow area midway requires at least 2 feet, and more is better; currents are fairly weak.

CAUTIONS: Mud, afternoon wind, and steep beach at mouth with channel to ocean sometimes open.

TRIP PLANNING: Paddle to mouth in morning to beat wind coming off the ocean; enjoy the tail wind on return—this is a great place for a sail rig.

LAUNCH SITE: From Highway 101 in Petaluma, take the East Washington Street exit and follow signs through town toward Bodega Bay; Washington turns into Bodega Avenue and then Highway 1. In Valley Ford, take a left at Dinucci's Italian Restaurant onto Valley Ford Estero. Cross the **bridge at Marin County Line,** take the next left onto Marsh Road and an immediate left on the short, bumpy driveway to the base of the bridge. Free, but limited parking (overnight okay); the generous boating etiquette dictates unloading gear at the launch then parking the car on the shoulder of the road. No facilities available.

Estero Americano

DIRECTIONS

START: Head west under the bridge, while bearing left along the bank. Not only will the route be obvious, but also why some refer to this stretch as the **muddy ditch**: The mud-bank channel is only as wide as your kayak is long. Have faith, the scenery soon improves. If the area at the put in is flooded (as it was for us on a recent early spring day on a strong El Niño year), the muddy ditch will be a broad pond, and the route will be ambiguous for the first 0.25 mile. Bear left and head for the dense copse of oaks 0.50 miles away on the left bank; the way will become clear as it narrows and winds between hills.

MILE 2.5: The channel widens and becomes shallower and often, windier as it bends right back to the west, rounding a **small islet** (inundated at very high water). Look for a landing spot along left bank. This makes a good turnaround if it's too windy, you're tired, or the tide is too low. *Caution:* You'll need at least 2 feet of tide to make it past this broad, shallow area. When in doubt, stay left for the next mile or so to find deeper water.

MILE 3.5: During high water, you may angle left into a **wide, shallow bay** and find a landing site. There is an old fishing boat left high and dry on the left bank near here.

MILE 4.25: The channel bends sharply left and narrows into a **steep valley,** now covered in coastal scrub, the best scenery so far.

MILE 5.5: There are dunes and sandbar at the estero mouth. This beach is the only public access point beyond the launch. The banks of the Estero are private property and should be treated with the same respect that you would ask of people in your yard. *Caution:* If the mouth is open, stay well left and land to avoid getting swept out to sea.

Where to Eat & Where to Stay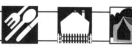

RESTAURANTS Dinucci's Italian Restaurant (707–876–3260) in Valley Ford serves hearty, family-style meals. **LODGING** Try **Valley Ford Hotel** (707–876–3600), about a block away from Dinucci's, simple and quiet. **CAMPING** **Bodega Dunes State Beach** on Highway 1 just north of Bodega Bay has sites in the dunes. (See also Route 10: North Tomales Bay.)

Estero Americano

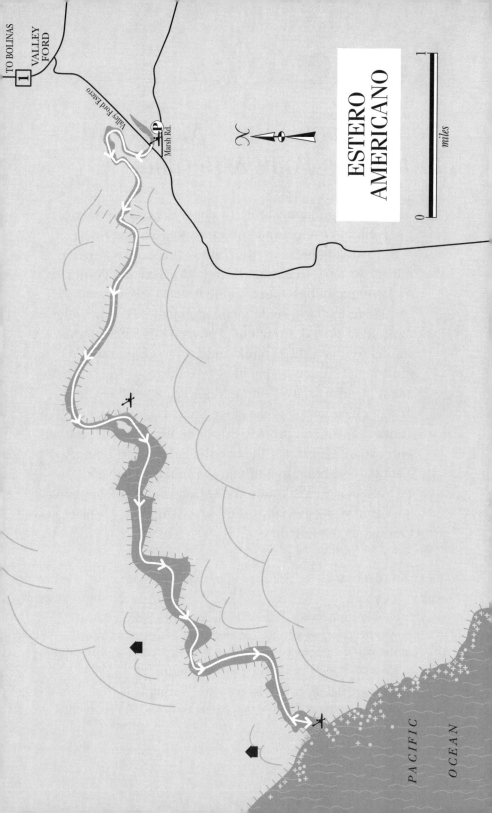

Route 10:

━━ ━━ ━━ ━━ ━━ ━━ ━━ ━━ ━━ ━━ ━━ ➤

North Tomales Bay—Nicks Cove to Tomales Point & Beyond

With its proximity to Point Reyes National Seashore, Nicks Cove provides access to some of the finest paddling in the greater San Francisco Bay Area. A mile or so across the water from Nicks, Tomales Point jabs a rocky finger 14 miles up into the Pacific—a giant, natural breakwater 500 feet high, forming Tomales Bay, the longest, most uninhabited, stretch of protected salt water on this coast. From behind its bluffs and beaches rise deserted, windswept hills, quilted golden green with coastal scrub and grassy meadows, laced with wildflowers. Several of the beaches have access to the ridge trail running the length of Tomales Point and provide excellent hiking opportunities, with expansive vistas of the bay, the Pacific, and Point Reyes National Seashore. In addition to numerous day-trip options, this area is known for its excellent kayak camping opportunities, especially for those looking to try overnight touring for the first time.

TRIP HIGHLIGHTS: Kayak camping, wildlife, hiking, and scenery.
TRIP RATING:

> *Beginner:* 4 miles along shore. Basic tide knowledge essential. Avoid afternoon winds and crossing the bay unless accompanied by an intermediate level trip leader, and you are comfortable paddling in 15- to 20-knot winds and 1- to 2-foot chop.

> *Intermediate:* 9 miles with bay crossing. Great place to get your feet wet kayak camping. Open-water rescue skills and tow rope highly

recommended. Surf zone practice at mouth of bay not recommended during ebb tide or when waves are bigger than 3 feet and winds above 15 knots.

Advanced/Expert: 15+ miles with open-coast sidetrip. Surfing and tide rips play at mouth of the bay. Access to rock gardens. Combat roll recommended. Begins to get dicey in swells greater than 6 feet and winds above 20 knots.

TRIP DURATION: Part day, full day, or overnight.

NAVIGATION AIDS: USGS: *Tomales Quadrangle* (7.5 minute), *Point Reyes National Seashore* map from Bear Valley Visitor Center, and NOAA chart 18643. Wx radio: "Point Arena to Pigeon Point"; buoys: Bodega Bay and Point Reyes.

TIDAL INFORMATION: Tides above 2 to 3 feet necessary to explore shallow areas over mudflats along the shallow, eastern half of the bay. Currents of 3 knots or more are possible during tide changes of 4 feet or more.

CAUTIONS: Dangerous waves and ocean-going currents around Sand Point at the mouth of the bay, especially during ebb tide; the bay's northwest orientation funnels afternoon winds, often 15 to 25 knots, which can quickly whip the bay into a froth of whitecaps and 1- to 2-foot chop in exposed areas, with waves becoming especially steep in shallow areas. If hiking on the point, stick to trails and beware of extensive poison oak thickets, ticks and, although rare, rattlesnakes in summer. Avoid disturbing seal haul outs and resting birds.

TRIP PLANNING: To take advantage of tidal currents, choose a day with a morning ebb tide and afternoon flood, which tends to put both wind and currents at your back on the return trip. Less-experienced paddlers can paddle before the winds kick up, cross the bay only at narrow points, or avoid crossings entirely. Mild fall weather provides the best camping and paddling conditions, but we've had calm, or crappy, weather here any time of year. To experience the solitude of Tomales Bay, midweek and off-season are best. On summer weekends, fishing skiffs ply the shore, zipping back and forth to check crab pots and occasionally stopping to picnic on the beaches; by sunset, however, the bay is generally quiet and deserted. As the popularity of kayak camping increases, so does competition for the bay's campsites; although a permit system is in the works (see Camping) sites are currently first come, first serve. Consider setting up early and sharing with other campers on summer weekends.

LAUNCH SITE: To reach Nicks from Highway 101 in the Bay Area head west on Sir Francis Drake Boulevard (five miles north of the Golden Gate Bridge in San Rafael) to Highway 1 North. About 10 miles north of Point Reyes Station you'll hit Nicks Cove (at Miller Landing County Park Boat Launch). Turn left into Nicks and continue past the boat ramp on your left for an easier launch off the kayakers' beach at the far northern end of the parking lot. Park there for day trips, being careful not to block the boat-trailer turnaround at the end of the road; for overnights, use the upper lot. Parking fees are $5.00/day, $10.00/overnight. Nicks has outhouses but no drinking water. If you travel from north of Petaluma on Highway 101, take the East Washington Street exit, head west to Bodega Avenue, which makes a funny hop across Petaluma Valley Ford Road to Tomales Road. So just keep heading west until you reach Highway 1. Then head south 4 miles and look for Nicks on your right. **Alternate launch site:** Lawson's Landing in Dillon Beach: $5.00 per day, or $12.00 overnight.

START: From **Nicks Cove** the most conservative route for beginners is to head northwest, hugging the shore past the ghost town remains of **Hamlet**.

MILE 1.0: The mudflat at the mouth of **Walker Creek** is among the bay's prime birding spots, especially for shorebirds and white pelicans. At low tide, stay 0.5 mile off shore, keeping to the west of the white stakes that mark the oyster beds, and head towards **Toms Point** (bearing 300°), which provides protection from both wind and incoming currents. *Sidetrip:* On blustery days, you can meander several miles up Walker Creek, with fair protection from the wind, but a high, incoming tide is recommended.

MILE 2.0: A good lunch stop at higher tides, **Toms Point** is also the narrowest place to cross the bay (just under 0.5 mile), offering less-experienced paddlers a good spot to reassess sea conditions before committing to a crossing. To avoid traffic, cross the boat channel (bearing 240°) without delay and hug the shoreline; because much of the bay is barely 6 feet deep, powerboats limit themselves to the narrow channel.

MILE 3.0: Several beach camps lie within 1 mile of Toms. To the south, the salt marsh at **Windy Gap** has the longest beach and is closest to the trailheads at White Gulch, but it offers little protection. Just north of Windy Gap, a narrow, unnamed beach at the base of the bluffs leaves barely enough room for a tent at high tide and no access to hiking. The **Eucalyptus Grove** (aka Ropeswing Camp) provides the best wind protection among the large eucalyptus and cypress by the rope swing, making it popular and typically the first to fill on busy weekends. Several small beaches at the base of the bluffs in this area, generally awash at high tide, make good rest stops. *Sidetrip:* From Nicks, an alternate, more exposed route is to cross to **Hog Island**, a picturesque speck of land covered in cypress trees a few hundred yards across. Overnight camping is no longer allowed on the island, and signs now limit landing to the western shore to protect wildlife. The backwaters of **White Gulch**, with broad mudflats that attract shorebirds, and a trailhead for hikes along the ridge crest are also worth a look. Time landings around high tide to avoid dragging your boat across acres of mud. This sidetrip adds 1 mile to the previous route.

MILE 4.0: The small sand beach at **Blue Gums** gives moderate protection for several tents and hiking access to the ridge trail running past stock ponds where elk sitings are common. Whether or not you see elk, the vistas of the Point Reyes Peninsula and the open sea from the ridge crest are outstanding, especially at sunset. *Caution:* When paddling near the mouth of Tomales Bay, be extremely wary of tide rips on outgoing tides and surf. In recent years, two fishing skiffs have been swept out the mouth and into heavy surf, resulting in several drownings—a fate that could easily befall an unprepared paddler, as it did in 1996 to a kayaker at the mouth of nearby Drakes Estero.

MILE 4.5: Avalis Beach has great views of Bodega Bay, the most room for camping, and good hiking access, but little wind protection.

MILE 5.5: A sidetrip to Tomales Point offers excellent ocean views for advanced intermediates in calm conditions. *Caution:* Ocean swells, breaking waves, winds, strong currents, and no landing options the last mile to the point make this area unsuitable for inexperienced paddlers.

MILE 6.5: *Caution:* The sidetrip around Tomales Point to **Bird Rock** is for advanced coastal kayakers only. Once around the point, prevailing winds can make return difficult. Boomers, cliffs, and large surf make landing all but impossible unless you have the skills to pick your way through the rock garden to the small beach in the lee of Bird Rock.

Native Tule Elk

In 1978, thirteen native Tule elk were reintroduced on Tomales Point. The herd now numbers about 500, making it one of the largest of the twenty-two herds in the state. The herd is thriving so well that wildlife managers are currently experimenting with elk contraception and transplanting herd members to other areas of the park in order to maintain an ecological balance. Fall promises the most exciting elk watching, as males are actively bugling, locking horns, and rutting.

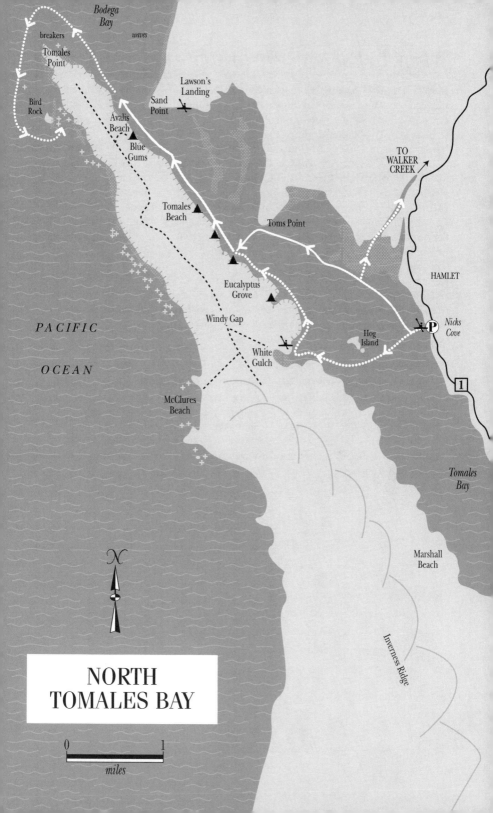

Bodega Bay

breakers

waves

Tomales
Point

Bird
Rock

Avalis
Beach

Sand
Point

Lawson's
Landing

Blue
Gums

Tomales
Beach

Toms Point

TO
WALKER
CREEK

HAMLET

*Nicks
Cove*

P

Eucalyptus
Grove

Windy Gap

White
Gulch

Hog
Island

1

PACIFIC

OCEAN

McClures
Beach

*Tomales
Bay*

Marshall
Beach

𝒩

Inverness Ridge

NORTH
TOMALES BAY

0   1

miles

Where to Eat & Where to Stay

RESTAURANTS   **Nick's Cove** (415–663–1033) next door to the launch site serves standard pub fare in the $5.00 to $10.00 range, featuring fresh fish and chips; the food's fair, but the views from the deck (and its proximity to the put in) are outstanding. **The Station House** (415–663–1515) on Highway 1 in Point Reyes Station has an excellent choice of fresh seafood, local oysters, and California cuisine in the $8.00 to $15.00 range.   **LODGING**   There are many cozy inns in the area: Contact the **West Marin Chamber of Commerce** (415–663–9232) or try the **West Marin Network** (415–663–9543) for a range of choices, from the **Point Reyes Youth Hostel** (415–663–8811) to the elegant **Point Reyes Seashore Lodge** (415–663–9000). **CAMPING**   For overnight camping on Tomales Point, the National Park Service now requires backcountry boat camping permits. This is the time to practice low-impact camping technique. No drinking water is available at campsites, so carry your own. Pit toilets are available only at Marshall and Tomales Beaches. All other camping beaches on Tomales Point are primitive with no facilities, and you are required to pack out *all* waste. This means that if you do not carry some sort of portable toilet, you can only get a permit to camp at Marshall or Tomales Beaches. For information, permits, and camping reservations contact Point Reyes National Seashore (415–663–8054). Reservations can be made up to three months in advance. For the latest information, call **Point Reyes National Seashore** (415–663–8054). **Samuel P. Taylor Park** (call Park Net for reservations at 800–444–7275) on Sir Francis Drake Boulevard has excellent stream-side sites beneath towering redwoods. **Olema Campground** (415–663–8001)—off Highway 1 south of Point Reyes Station—is closer to the bay but less scenic with family camping and hookups in a grassy meadow. **Lawson's Landing** (707–878–2443), located at the mouth of the bay in Dillon Beach, has excellent launch access, but campsites are scattered across a treeless pasture often crowded with RVs and the occasional wandering cow. All three campgrounds have toilets and hot showers.

Route 11:

■ ■ ■ ■ ■ ■ ■ ■ ■ ■ ■ ■ ■ ■ ■ ➤

Central Tomales Bay— Inverness to Hog Island

With its access to numerous flatwater day trips as well as overnight camping on the Point Reyes National Seashore, Central Tomales Bay is a favorite choice of local paddlers. As you paddle from Inverness toward the more exposed northern part of the bay, conditions become gradually more challenging. The first 3 miles to Indian Beach is well protected and scenic, following high bluffs that are cloaked in a forest of Bishop pines and punctuated every half mile or so by a sandy beach. Around Marshall Beach, the pine forest gives way to the brushy grasslands and the steep, rolling hills of Tomales Point. From here on the bay begins to widen slightly and campsites become available.

TRIP HIGHLIGHTS: Excellent birding, protected water, scenery, and camping.

TRIP RATING:

Beginner: 1–15 miles. On calm days with winds to 10 knots, energetic beginners might make it all the way to Hog Island. On rougher days, the 6–mile round-trip to Indian Beach makes a good day trip. Bay crossings not recommended unless accompanied by intermediate paddlers in winds below 15 knots.

Intermediate: 6–15+ miles possible in winds 15 to 20 knots. Bay crossings not recommended unless experienced performing open-water rescues.

TRIP DURATION: Part day, full day, overnight, or multiday.

NAVIGATION AIDS: USGS: *Pt. Reyes National Seashore and Vicinity* (15 minute) and *Tomales Quadrangle* (7.5 minute), *Point Reyes*

National Seashore map from Bear Valley Visitor Center, and NOAA chart 18643. Wx radio: "Point Arena to Pigeon Point"; buoys: Bodega Bay and Point Reyes.

TIDAL INFORMATION: More landing options if not high tide; currents become stronger farther north.

CAUTIONS: Mud flats, currents, afternoon wind, restricted swimming areas, and private beaches.

TRIP PLANNING: Paddle north with a morning outgoing tide and return with the incoming tide and the wind at your back. Stay close to shore for better wind protection, contouring your route behind points of land to take advantage of wind shadows. If planning to camp, see launch sites (following) for those that allow overnight parking.

LAUNCH SITE: To reach Inverness from Highway 101 in San Rafael, head west on Sir Francis Drake Boulevard (5 miles north of Golden Gate Bridge) and turn right where it joins Highway 1 North in Olema. Just south of Point Reyes Station, turn left off Highway 1 to stay on Sir Francis Drake where it heads west again at the sign for Tomales Bay State Park. In Inverness, just after Golden Hinde Inn & Marina and Blue Waters Kayaking (415–669–2600) on the right, you will see a large pullout and an outhouse across from Pine Hill Drive. This is Chicken Ranch launch site. No fee, outhouse, overnight parking okay. **Alternate launch sites:** Hearts Desire State Beach (no overnight parking, $5.00 day-use fee, fresh water); to reach it follow signs through Inverness to Tomales Bay State Park, turn right on Pierce Point Road and right again into the state park at Hearts Desire Beach. Easier to get to is the Golden Hinde Inn & Marina, but they charge $10 for launching. Across the bay on Highway 1, you can park overnight at Marshall (not Marshall Beach) or Nicks Cove (see rte. 10). There is day parking at Millerton Park on Highway 1, 4 miles north of Point Reyes Station (launch from Alan Sieroty Beach on south side of park, best at nearly high tide); free parking, outhouse.

DIRECTIONS

START: Head north along bluffs from **Chicken Ranch**. *Caution:* During summer stay outside of swimming areas marked by buoys, and don't

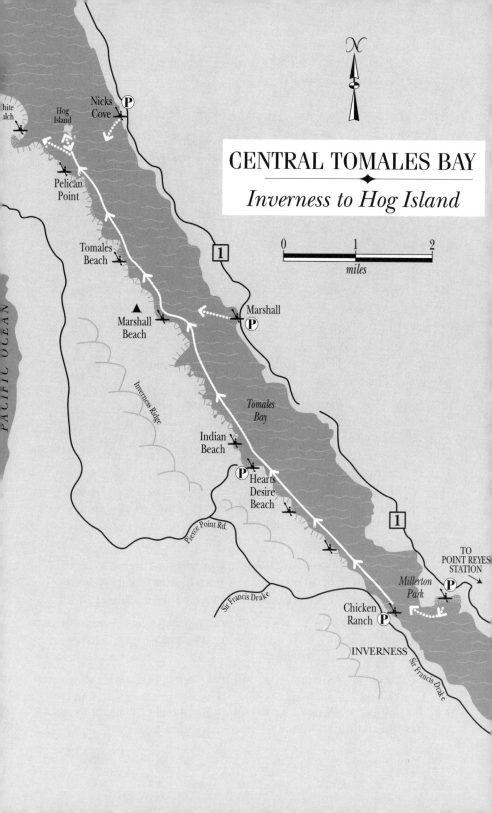

land on private docks or beaches. Among the several small beaches for the next 3 miles, landings are permitted only on those with brown state park signs.

MILE 2.5: **Hearts Desire Beach** makes a good alternate launch site to access the beaches farther north; launching and landing allowed to far south side of swimming beach.

MILE 3.0: When you spot the *kotcas,* the Miwok bark dwellings that look like wooden teepees, you'll know you've found **Indian Beach.** As the site of an original village, the beach makes an interesting rest stop. In addition to the recreated dwellings, the beach has a self-guided natural history trail that winds through the forest to the south, and the lagoon behind the beach has good birding. This makes a good turn-around spot on windy days as exposure to wind and currents increases beyond. If you continue around the point, look for Pelican Point and Hog Island in the distance.

MILE 5.0: You've crossed from state park property to the national seashore. Shoreline camping is allowed from here at **Marshall Beach** (the only campsite on the bay with pit toilets) to Tomales Point.

MILE 6.0: **Tomales Beach** has a primitive campsite. A near continuous mile of sandy beach to the north allows good landing options except at high tide.

MILE 7.0: **Pelican Point** makes a good landmark and landing. *Sidetrips:* Another campsite lies 0.5 mile past the point. (For information on Hog Island [another 0.75 mile] and the campsites of North Tomales Bay, see rte. 10.)

Central Tomales Bay

Coastal Miwok:
The First Local Paddlers

The name Tomales has nothing to do with Mexican food. In the tongue of the original Miwok inhabitants, *tamal* means bays. Early settlers added the word bay to Tomales. So essentially the name Tomales Bay translates to *bays bay*. These bay people took full advantage of their fertile waterfront location, harvesting a bounty of waterfowl, fish, and shellfish. The Miwok were also the area's first paddlers. They fished and hunted from kayaklike boats called *saka*, made from bundles of reeds lashed together at the ends. When these disposable boats became waterlogged, the Miwok simply gathered up another bundle of reeds and whipped up a new one.

Where to Eat & Where to Stay

RESTAURANTS   A couple of reasonably priced yet hearty spots in Point Reyes Station are **Bovine Bakery** (415–663–9420) and **Cafe Reyes** (415–663–9493). **Perry's Deli** (415–663–1491) in Inverness Park makes great fresh sandwiches and snacks to go. In Inverness try **Gray Whale Pub and Pizzeria** (415–669–1244) or **Inverness Store** (415–669–1041). **LODGING**   **Dancing Coyote**, one of many bed and breakfasts in the area, has a good launch beach (415–669–7200). For a splurge, try **Manka's Inverness Lodge & Restaurant** (415–669–1034). For less expensive digs with launch access, try **Golden Hinde Inn & Marina** (800–339–9398 in California or 415–669–1389). Or try reservation service through **West Marin Network** (415–663–9543). **CAMPING**   Except for Marshall Beach, camping on Tomales Point is primitive with no facilities. (See Route 10: North Tomales for latest permit information and other campgrounds.)

Route 12:

South Tomales Bay—White House Pool to Millerton Park

The well-protected first section of this trip winds along a creek at the northern edge of Olema Marsh, a dense alder-willow thicket providing one of the most diverse bird habitats in the area, where the range of migrant land birds overlaps that of waterfowl. Gradually the creek's tree-lined banks open up to reeds, then salt marsh, and finally into the broad expanse of south Tomales Bay, offering nice views of pine-forested Inverness Ridge along the left and rolling coastal hills on the right. Birding is good along the entire route. Ducks, geese, and shorebirds abound in the marsh, and Millerton Park harbors an osprey nesting site.

TRIP HIGHLIGHTS: Excellent birding and protected water.

TRIP RATING:

Beginner: 1–8 mile round-trip to Millerton Park on days with high tide and low wind, i.e., 3–4 feet and less than 15 knots; ability to read a tide book essential.

Intermediate: 8-mile round-trip to Millerton can get choppy in strong wind.

TRIP DURATION: Part day.

NAVIGATION AIDS: USGS: *Point Reyes National Seashore and Vicinity* (15 minute), *Point Reyes National Seashore* map from Bear Valley Visitor Center, and NOAA chart 18643. Wx radio: "Point Arena to Pigeon Point"; buoys: Bodega Bay and Point Reyes.

TIDAL INFORMATION: When tides are below 3–4 feet, mud blocks access to Tomales Bay within 1–2 miles of the launch site, and the creek may be too shallow to paddle.

CAUTIONS: Mud, wind, and confusing channels.

TRIP PLANNING: Pick a day with a high, rising tide, and paddle early before the wind picks up (or do shuttle and one-way trip). Be sure to return before the tide drops.

LAUNCH SITE: From Highway 101 in San Rafael, head west on Sir Francis Drake (5 miles north of Golden Gate Bridge) and turn right where it joins Highway 1 North in Olema. Just south of Point Reyes Station, turn left off Highway 1 to stay on Sir Francis Drake where it heads west again at the sign for Tomales Bay State Park. Take the first right into parking lot for White House Pool. Free parking; pit toilets available. Other launch sites: Alan Sieroty Beach on the south side of Millerton Park on Highway 1, 4 miles north of Point Reyes Station; free parking, outhouses.

DIRECTIONS

START: The mud bank at the put in at **White House Pool,** which can be a little awkward, is one of the more challenging aspects of this easy first section. Head left along the narrow, tree-lined channel. *Sidetrip:* At high tide you can paddle right for a mile or more up the creek past Point Reyes Station.

MILE 0.25: The channel bends right—north—soon leaving the trees.

MILE 0.75: A midstream islet allows a landing spot, as do several beaches along the left bank, if you're careful about the mud and trampling sensitive marsh plants. *Caution:* The channel begins to silt up from here on, so be sure you have enough tide left to continue.

MILE 2.0: The channel banks end and the bay opens up to nearly 1 mile wide, making it a good turn-around point for less-energetic paddlers. To continue look for the knoll of **Millerton Point** (compass bearing 300°) another 1.5 miles in the distance. Although you'll eventually angle right toward the base of the point, aim for the point for the next mile or so to stay in deeper water, following a line of wooden stakes. *Caution:* If you continue on, look back to memorize the correct channel so that you can find it on your return. If you have a Global Positioning System (GPS), mark a waypoint **(N 38° 05' 30", W 122° 50' 04")**.

MILE 3.75: The first clump of trees to the right of Millerton Point is **Alan Sieroty Beach,** a good landing spot with an outhouse. The platform atop a pole supports an osprey nest.

Where to Eat & Where to Stay

RESTAURANTS AND LODGING See Route 11: Central Tomales. **CAMPING** See Route 10: North Tomales Bay.

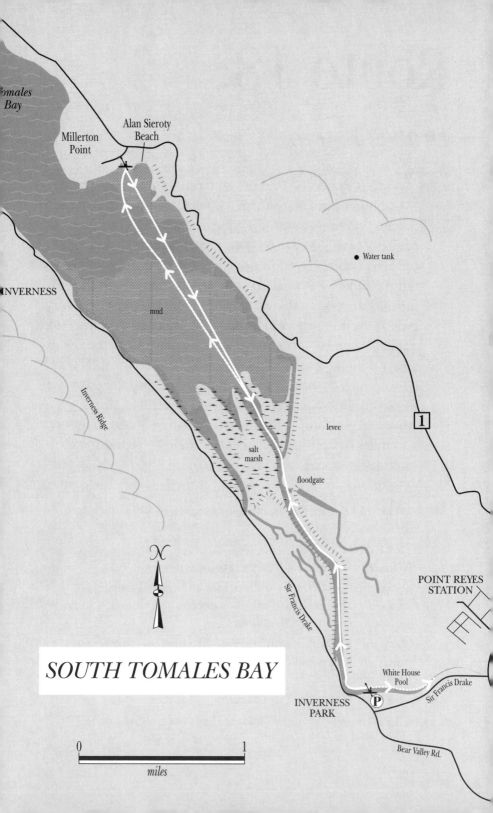

*omales
Bay*

Millerton
Point

Alan Sieroty
Beach

● Water tank

INVERNESS

mud

Inverness Ridge

levee

salt
marsh

floodgate

1

N

Sir Francis Drake

POINT REYES
STATION

SOUTH TOMALES BAY

White House
Pool

P

Sir Francis Drake

INVERNESS
PARK

0   1

miles

Bear Valley Rd.

Route 13:

━━ ━ ━ ━ ━ ━ ━ ━ ━ ━ ━ ━ ━━▶

Drakes Estero

The four fingers of Drakes Estero and the double thumb of Limantour Estero form a 20-mile network of narrow bays that presses into the marshy center of Point Reyes National Seashore like a giant, deformed handprint. The only road access is at Johnson's Oyster Farm at the tip of the middle finger, a 3.5-mile paddle across the palm to the sea. Beyond the put in, the estero feels quiet and remote. The only access to its shores is by boat or trail, and no motorized craft are allowed (except the working boats from the oyster farm). Rolling grassy hills surround the waterways. Here curious harbor seals shadow your strokes, and the estuary's fertile mudflats attract a wide variety of birdlife. For advanced paddlers Drakes Estero provides access to miles and miles of uninhabited ocean shoreline, permitting a multiday camping tour (see rte. 15).

TRIP HIGHLIGHTS: Peaceful, remote, with good birding and harbor seal watching.

TRIP RATING:

Beginner: 1–20 miles of shallow, protected water.

Intermediate: 1–20 miles with surfing and coastal touring possibilities for those with previous experience, when it's a flood tide and waves are less than 3 feet.

Advanced: 1–20 miles with access to surf and coastal touring; launch site for coastal camping tours (see Route 15: Drakes Bay to Coast Camp).

TRIP DURATION: Part or full day.

NAVIGATION AIDS: USGS: *Point Reyes National Seashore and*

Vicinity (15 minute), *Point Reyes National Seashore* map from Bear Valley Visitor Center, and NOAA chart 18647. Wx radio: "Point Arena to Pigeon Point"; buoys: Bodega Bay, Point Reyes, and S.E. Farallon Island.

TIDAL INFORMATION: Extensive mudflats begin to uncover below 2 feet, and the launch beach gets muddy below 3 feet. Strong currents at mouth.

CAUTIONS: Drakes Estero and Limantour Spit closed to boating March 15 to June 30. Mud, strong afternoon winds, and dangerous currents at the mouth during ebb tide.

TRIP PLANNING: Except at the mouth, tide height is more of a concern in this shallow estuary than tidal currents. Although it's often possible to find channels around the mudflats during low tides, a high, rising tide simplifies route finding and makes the launch beach less muddy. Strong afternoon winds tend to funnel down Schooner Bay toward the mouth so head back early or save some energy for the return; use the bluffs as wind breaks whenever possible. We have heard of several instances of paddlers, unable to make progress against the wind, having to abandon their boats and hike out, so check your weather radio for a day when wind is less than 15 knots.

LAUNCH SITE: To reach Johnson's Oyster Farm from Highway 101 in San Rafael, head west on Sir Francis Drake Highway (5 miles north of Golden Gate Bridge) and turn right where it joins Highway 1 North in Olema. Just south of Point Reyes Station, turn left off Highway 1 to stay on Sir Francis Drake where it heads west again at the sign for Tomales Bay State Park. Continue past Inverness 4 miles into the park, then turn left at the sign for Johnson's. Just before you reach the buildings, park on the right near the water. Free parking; no facilities (but you may be able to use the farm's bathroom if you buy some fresh oysters).

DIRECTIONS

START: From **Johnson's Oyster Farm** paddle along the steep left bank out of Schooner Bay.

MILE 1.5: The estero widens at the mouth of **Home Bay.** *Sidetrips:*

Explore the 1-mile length of Home Bay on your left or cross to the right shore and head 1.5 miles into narrow Creamery Bay. *Caution:* Be careful not to spook the harbor seals hauled out throughout the estero from this point on.

MILE 2.5: The estero narrows again, and the hillsides steepen around **Barries Bay**, the smallest "finger" off Drakes Estero. *Sidetrip:* Narrow Barries Bay extends 1 mile.

MILE 3.5: Land to the far right of the **mouth of Drakes Estero** in a small cove at the end of the bluffs. This makes a good lunch stop, with a picnic table and some wind protection; a short walk across the sand spit reveals good views of Drakes Bay and the Pacific. *Caution:* Be careful around the mouth for two reasons: to avoid disturbing the seals hauled out on the left at the end of Limantour Spit, and to avoid ebb currents, which can be dangerous—one kayaker has been swept out into the surf and drowned here. *Sidetrip:* On calm days experienced coastal paddlers can find good surf and coastal touring to Drakes Beach or down the coast to Coast Camp and beyond (see rte. 15). *Caution:* Scout conditions from the shore first: Tide rips, rip currents, and heavy surf are common at the mouth.

MILE 5.0: Continue into **Limantour Estero** to the mouth of its main bay. Turn left to explore it or head straight along Limantour Spit. Both options are another mile to the end.

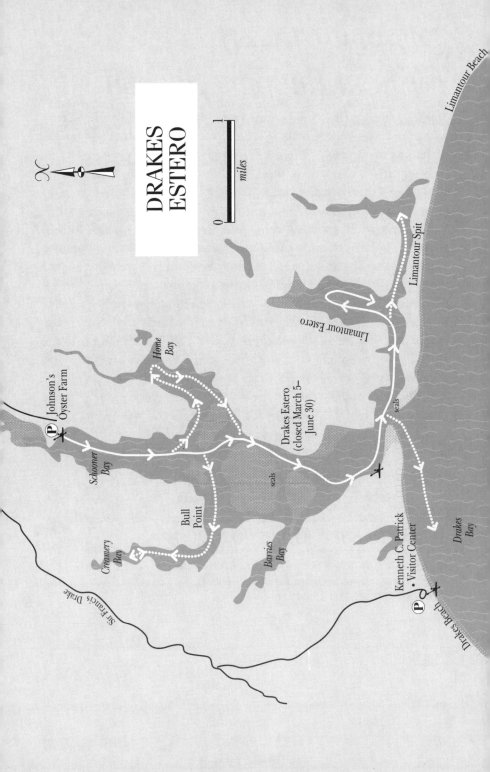

DRAKES
ESTERO

0 — 1
miles

Limantour Beach

Limantour Spit

Limantour Estero

seals

Drakes Estero
(closed March 5–
June 30)

seals

Home
Bay

Johnson's
Oyster Farm

Schooner
Bay

Bull
Point

Creamery
Bay

Barries
Bay

Sir Francis Drake

Kenneth C. Patrick
Visitor Center

Drakes
Bay

Drakes Beach

Drakes Closed for Seal-Pupping Season

Drakes Estero is closed to boating from March 15 through June 30 to allow the area's harbor seals *(Phoca vitulina)* to bear their young free of human disturbance. The pups, able to swim at birth, are just 2 feet long and weigh about 20 pounds. But their size doubles within a month on a diet of seal milk that is nearly 50 percent fat. When Drakes reopens, it's important to stay 100 yards or more from seal haul outs to avoid spooking the colony. Seals haul out on land to warm up because they are unable to maintain their body temperature if they remain in the water all the time. Not only will the animals get cold if frightened into the water, but pups sometimes become separated from their mothers or even crushed by stampeding adults. Watch for movement among the resting animals, when you see their heads rise, you are too close—time to back paddle or move off to the side. There are volunteers with high-powered telescopes monitoring the seals; kayakers can get cited for flushing seals off their resting beaches. If you find a pup on the beach, leave it alone, chances are it is not abandoned. Mothers often leave pups ashore while hunting, but they won't return if humans are around. The best thing to do is leave the area and report the location to park rangers, who can then call marine mammal rescue personnel for any truly deserted pups.

Where to Eat & Where to Stay

RESTAURANTS, LODGING, & CAMPING Fresh oysters from **Johnson's Oyster Farm** (415–669–1149). (See also Route 10: North Tomales and Route 11: Central Tomales.)

Route 14:

■■ ■■ ■■ ■■■ ■■ ■■■ ■■ ■■ ■■ ■■ ➤

Drakes Beach to Chimney Rock & the Point Reyes Headlands

Although Spanish explorer Don Sebastian Vizcaino named the massive headland here "Kings Point" because the day in 1603 that he first laid eyes on it was the Feast of the Three Kings, Point Reyes lives up to its regal title any day of the year. Literally one of the more outstanding points on the California coast, Point Reyes punches a rocky right fist into the Pacific—with its thumb sticking out and down. Below the point, the semisheltered crescent of Drakes Beach, which in this fist analogy stretches down the lower wrist to the thumb tip, is the most-protected ocean front beach on the entire Point Reyes National Seashore, making it the best place in the park to gain coastal touring experience. Several miles of flat sandy beach fringes the base of the bluffs at low tide, providing both good landing access through (generally) small surf and fine scenery. At the far end of the beach, the chalky sandstone cliffs of Drakes Bay give way to the craggy granite knuckles of the Point Reyes Headlands, a 3-mile seawall of 400-foot cliffs that, for experienced paddlers, provides one of the most dynamic and dramatic roundings on the West Coast.

TRIP HIGHLIGHTS: Solitude and excellent scenery and surfing.

TRIP RATING:

Beginner: 1–6 mile round-trip as far as Chimney Rock for advanced beginners accompanied by an intermediate paddler on a day with surf less than 1 foot at Drakes Beach and winds to 10 knots.

Intermediate: 1–6+ miles with good surf zone practice for those with previous coastal touring experience on days with surf to 3 feet and winds below 15 knots. It's not recommended that you go beyond Chimney Rock without advanced leadership.

Advanced: 6–10+ miles along Point Reyes Headlands with landing possible beyond the lighthouse if surf on exposed South Beach is below 4–6 feet. (Although it's possible to paddle the headlands in swells in excess of 10 feet, it's difficult to appreciate the scenery in seas above 6 feet.)

TRIP DURATION: Part to full day.

NAVIGATION AIDS: USGS: *Point Reyes National Seashore and Vicinity* (15 minute), *Point Reyes National Seashore* map from Bear Valley Visitor Center, and NOAA chart 18647. Wx radio: "Point Arena to Pigeon Point"; buoys: Bodega Bay, Point Reyes, and S.E. Farallon Island.

TIDAL INFORMATION: Lower tides leave better beach access along cliffs.

CAUTIONS: Afternoon, offshore wind; surf; submerged rocks; and fog. Although the beach's southerly exposure gives it good protection from prevailing seas, wind whipping over the peninsula can create dangerous offshore conditions if you stray too far from shore. Beach closures at mouth of Drakes Estero. Extreme exposure beyond Chimney Rock.

TRIP PLANNING: Although you can usually land between Drakes Beach and Chimney Rock except at high tide, more beach will be exposed along cliffs on days when tides are lower. These cliffs provide some protection, so stay close to shore to minimize the effects of offshore winds; this will be easier to do on a day with smaller surf.

Drakes Beach to Chimney Rock

LAUNCH SITE: To reach Drakes Beach from Highway 101 in San Rafael, head west on Sir Francis Drake (5 miles north of Golden Gate Bridge) and turn right where it joins Highway 1 North in Olema. Just south of Point Reyes Station, turn left off Highway 1 to stay on Sir Francis Drake where it heads west again at the sign for Tomales Bay State Park. Continue through Inverness and past Drakes Estero toward Point Reyes Lighthouse, turning left at the sign for Drakes Beach and the Kenneth C. Patrick Visitor Center. Free parking, rest rooms, and water available. **Alternate launch site:** Johnson's Oyster Farm (see Route 13: Drakes Estero).

DIRECTIONS

START: Paddle southwest along the cliffs and the long sweep of **Drakes Beach**. *Caution:* Stay close to shore to reduce your exposure to offshore winds. *Sidetrips:* Head east toward the mouth of Drakes Estero and beyond. *Caution:* Exposure to wind and surf increases as you continue toward the estero (see rte. 15). Drakes Estero and Limantour Spit are closed March 15–June 30.

MILE 2.0: The gentle curve of beach angles hard left just before the **fishing pier**. *Caution:* Do not approach if elephant seals are present.

MILE 3.0: **Chimney Rock**, at the southeast tip of Point Reyes, makes a good turn-around point. On calm days you may be able to round the point for a peek at the wave-pounded headlands. *Caution:* Extreme exposure beyond Chimney Rock. For experienced coastal paddlers, the next 3 miles of cliffs to the lighthouse is spectacular. On calm days rock garden paddling is possible but don't expect to land: The few beaches may be claimed by elephant seals.

MILE 6.0+: *Caution:* Landing on the northwest-facing beach beyond **Point Reyes Lighthouse** is not recommended unless scouted first from the South Beach parking lot and it's a very calm day: **Point Reyes Beach** is among the roughest, most-exposed beaches in the state.

Where to Eat & Where to Stay

RESTAURANTS Try **Drakes Beach Cafe** (415–669–1297) the park concession at the put in. (Or see Route 12: South Tomales Bay). **LODGING AND CAMPING** See Route 12: South Tomales Bay

Drakes Beach to Chimney Rock

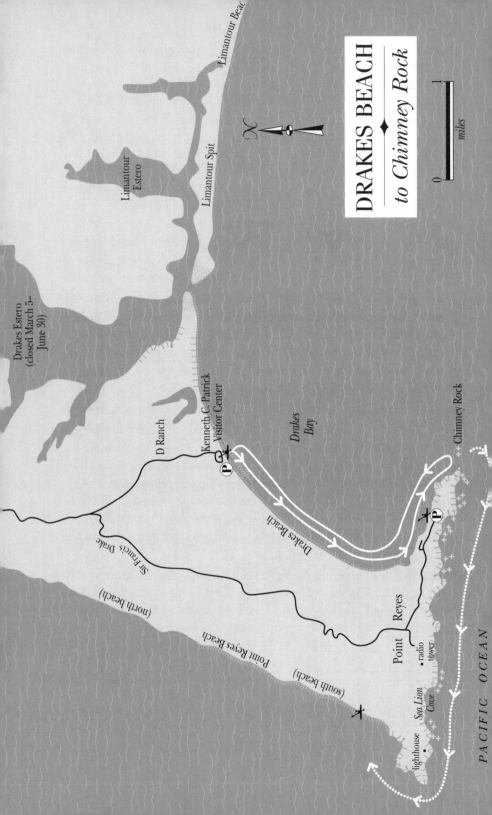

DRAKES BEACH
to Chimney Rock

miles

0   1

Limantour Beach

Limantour Spit

Limantour Estero

Drakes Estero
(closed March 5–
June 30)

D Ranch

Kenneth C. Patrick
Visitor Center

Drakes Bay

Sir Francis Drake

(north beach)

Point Reyes Beach

(south beach)

Drakes Beach

Point Reyes

radio tower

lighthouse

Sea Lion Cove

Chimney Rock

PACIFIC OCEAN

Paddling the Headlands:
The Two Faces of Point Reyes

I first paddled the headlands in 1992, while scouting a whale-watching tour. Knowing that the waters below the lighthouse were among the best places in California to see migrating grays from shore, my business partner at that time had set up a tour for intermediate paddlers, although neither of us had paddled the area before. We launched from the Chimney Rock fishing pier through small surf on a April afternoon to figure out the best route for that weekend. When we rounded the point at Chimney Rock, the full force of the 10- to 12-foot seas and 20-knot winds met us head on. The conditions forced us to stay 0.5 mile or more from shore where frightening walls of surf boomed against the cliffs. After fifteen minutes of struggling into the wind and bouncing in confused seas, able to steal only quick glances at the scenery, we retreated back to the shelter of the point, certain that weekend's whale-watching tour would be a bust. When Saturday rolled around, our trusting flock followed us out around Chimney Rock to the open Pacific, where they "oohed" and "aahed," setting paddles across their laps as they snapped photos of the towering headlands in uncommonly calm seas. Feeling incredibly lucky, we skirted close to shore behind sea stacks and past elephant seal colonies that two days earlier had been engulfed in raging foam. And though they must have been there, we saw no whales—everyone was so spellbound by the scenery toward shore, we apparently forgot to look.

Route 15:

▬▬ ▬▬ ▬▬ ▬▬ ▬▬ ▬▬ ▬▬ ▬▬ ▬▬ ▬▬ ▬▬ ⟶

Point Reyes National Seashore Outer Coast Camping Tour—Drakes Bay to Coast Camp & Beyond

One of the premier open-coast camping trips in the state, the lower half of the Point Reyes National Seashore is a southerly version of Mendocino's Lost Coast: a 20-mile stretch of roadless, uninhabited coastal wilderness, with rugged cliffs and remote beaches, providing an ample challenge for the most experienced paddlers. It is possible to do just the upper section as an overnighter, 8 miles each way to Coast Camp and back, and skip the messy shuttle logistics. Or go for the full effect and paddle the entire 24 miles down to Stinson Beach in three days. Either way you'll pass some of the wildest coastal real estate in the country, as its "National Seashore" designation would suggest.

TRIP HIGHLIGHTS: Open-coast camping, rock gardens, Solitude with a capital S, and scenery.

TRIP RATING:

Intermediate: 16-mile round-trip to Coast Camp and back for those with previous coastal touring experience in waves below 4 feet and winds to 15 knots. Because of the exposure, advanced trip leader is recommended.

Advanced: 16-mile round-trip or 24 miles one way to Stinson Beach; surf landings difficult in waves greater than 6 feet; rough seas in winds above 20 knots.

TRIP DURATION: Overnight(s).

NAVIGATION AIDS: USGS: *Point Reyes National Seashore and Vicinity*

(15 minute), *Point Reyes National Seashore* map from Bear Valley Visitor Center, and NOAA chart 18647. Wx radio: "Point Arena to Pigeon Point"; buoys: Bodega Bay, Point Reyes, and S.E. Farallon Island.

TIDAL INFORMATION: Tides above 2 to 3 feet necessary to get through Drakes Estero; lower tides on open coast leave more beaches exposed for landing.

CAUTIONS: Drakes Estero closed to kayaking March 15–June 30. Standard open-coast hazards: fog, strong afternoon winds, boomers, rough seas, and surf landings. Extreme exposure: When camping overnight en route, worsening conditions could leave you stranded, forcing a long hike out without your boat.

TRIP PLANNING: Paddle early, wind and seas tend to get worse in afternoon. Bring extra food and be prepared for weather layovers. Camping within the seashore, permitted only in established sites at Coast and Wildcat Camps, requires backcountry permit from park service (see Camping). If returning to Drakes Estero, head north early to beat the wind. If going all the way to Stinson Beach, park shuttle vehicle on side street in town, then walk out the shortcut trail from north side of town onto state beach and identify some landmarks, so you'll be able to find the closest place to land at journey's end.

LAUNCH SITE: Johnson's Oyster Farm (see rte. 13); free parking, no facilities. **Alternate launch site:** Drakes Beach (see rte. 14). Overnight parking prohibited. Landing site: Stinson State Beach on Highway 1 in Stinson Beach (overnight parking in town).

DIRECTIONS

START: From **Johnson's Oyster Farm**, paddle out Drakes Estero (see rte. 13).

MILE 3.5: The sandspit at the **mouth of Drakes Estero** is a good place to land and assess sea conditions before committing yourself to the open ocean (but try not to disturb any seals hauled out on Limantour Spit). *Caution:* Tide rips, rip currents, and heavy surf are common off the mouth of Drakes; at least one kayaker has drowned here.

MILE 8.0: 1 mile past where the bluffs start at the end of Limantour Spit

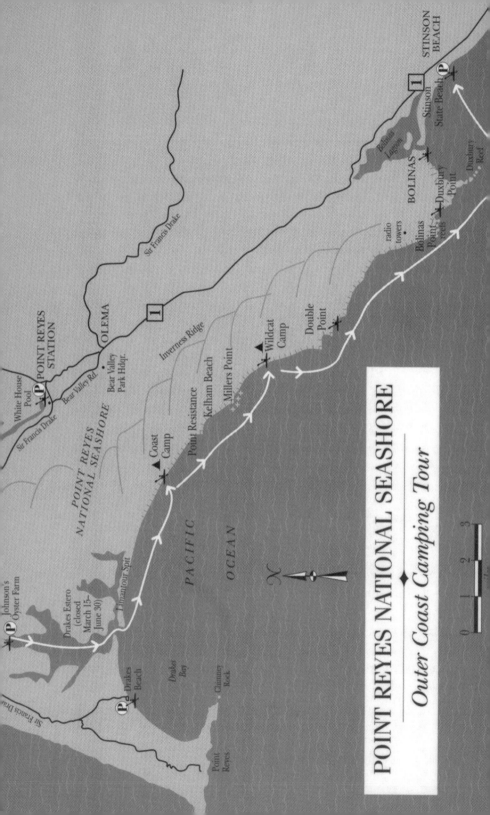

POINT REYES NATIONAL SEASHORE
Outer Coast Camping Tour

PACIFIC OCEAN

STINSON BEACH

Stinson State Beach

Bolinas Lagoon

BOLINAS

Duxbury Reef

Bolinas Point – Duxbury reefs

Bolinas Point

radio towers

Double Point

Wildcat Camp

Millers Point

Kelham Beach

Point Resistance

Coast Camp

Inverness Ridge

POINT REYES NATIONAL SEASHORE

Bear Valley Park Hdqr.

Bear Valley Rd.

OLEMA

Sir Francis Drake

POINT REYES STATION

White House Pool

Sir Francis Drake

Johnson's Oyster Farm

Drakes Estero (closed March 15–June 30)

Limantour Spit

Drakes Beach

Drakes Bay

Chimney Rock

Point Reyes

Sir Francis Drake

0   1   2   3

is the beach below **Coast Camp**. It's a long carry uphill to the campground. If you leave your boat down on the beach, be sure it's secure from marauding raccoons and well above the tide line. *Caution:* Carefully reassess sea conditions before continuing down the coast. It's only 5 miles of open water back to the mouth of Drakes Estero but an increasingly exposed, 16-mile commitment to Stinson Beach.

MILE 11.0: If it's calm enough, you might try the rock gardens off **Millers Point**.

MILE 12.5: Look for **Wildcat Camp** atop a flat bluff just past the steepest section of cliffs so far. *Caution:* The beach here is steep and exposed.

MILE 14.5: Cove at **Double Point** has landing possibilities at lower tides, but the beach below the south point is more protected.

MILE 19.0: *Caution:* The gently sloping sand beaches in the lee of **Bolinas Point** are less exposed than those to the north, but reefs can make for interesting landings, creating both protection and rocky hazards, depending on swell and tide height.

MILE 21.0: Conditions should get calmer beyond **Duxbury Point**. *Caution:* **Duxbury Reef,** an amazing and potentially hazardous land form (see later), stretches its rocky grasp nearly 1 mile out to sea. If the tide is high and the swell is low, you might paddle right over the reef next to shore without noticing it. But if the tide is down and the swell high, you'll need to detour well out to sea beyond the wave-pounded rocks early, before the prevailing winds blow you into danger.

MILE 24.0: Look for lifeguard towers and any other landmarks to find your landing spot on **Stinson State Beach.**

Point Reyes National Seashore

Duxbury Reef

North America's largest shale reef, Duxbury is renowned among local marine biologists for the diversity of its intertidal life. During minus tides, it is possible to explore tide pools several hundred yards out on the reef. Beyond the common pools of mussels, hermit crabs, sea anemones, and sea stars lies the rarely seen realm of the lower tidal zones, normally submerged beneath the waves. Here abalone cling to the rocks beside giant gumboot chiton, sea cucumbers, and, for the careful observer, a variety of colorful nudibranchs.

Where to Eat & Where to Stay

RESTAURANTS   **Parkside Cafe** (415–868–1272), adjacent to Stinson State Beach, is a good option if you want to grab a bite before heading back to Drakes Estero for your shuttle car. There are several other options on Highway 1. (See Route 12: White House Pool for food near Point Reyes.)   **LODGING**   (See Route 12: White House Pool and Route 16: Bolinas Lagoon.)   **CAMPING**   To reserve backcountry permits, call **Point Reyes National Seashore** (415–663–8054); cost is $10/night, and on summer weekends, sites book quickly within the two-month reservation period. Campgrounds have water and outhouses.

Route 16:

▬ ▬ ▬ ▬ ▬ ▬ ▬ ▬ ▬ ▬ ▬ ▬ ▬ ▬ ▬ ➤

Bolinas Lagoon & Duxbury Reef

A bird-watcher's dream, this shallow, salt marsh lagoon at the wild southern edge of Point Reyes National Seashore is simple to paddle at high tide, when much of its 2-mile length is accessible. At low tide, however, the extensive mudflats that hungry migratory birds find so enticing limit boating to narrow channels. Besides mud, a potential sticking point to paddling here may be its proximity to the backwater bohemian burg of Bolinas. Although most Bolinians are outwardly friendly, they prefer life off the beaten path, and undercurrents of reclusiveness persist—evidenced by the fact that no sign on Highway 1 marks the turnoff to their quiet village because locals tear it down. The desire for solitude (captured in a tongue-in-cheek bumper sticker we saw there recently which read, "Why do they call it 'tourist season' if you're not allowed to shoot them?") seems to stem from respect for their surroundings, an honest yearning not to have their peaceful and picturesque spot overrun by uncaring outsiders. There are rumblings afoot to ban paddling in the lagoon because in the past some unwitting boaters have scared seals off haul outs and frightened migratory waterfowl off the water (see later). Therefore maintaining a low profile (we recommend launch sites along Highway 1 to ease parking pressures in town) and a respectful attitude toward wildlife may be essential to continued access for kayakers. Beyond the lagoon the sandbar off its mouth is a popular place to practice kayak surfing in the often gentle waves, and the protection of Duxbury reef, the largest shale reef in North America, makes it a good spot for introductory coastal touring on calm days.

TRIP HIGHLIGHTS: Excellent bird watching, seals, protection, access to surfing, and semiprotected coastal touring.

TRIP RATING:

Beginner: 1–4 miles of protected water at high tide.

Intermediate: 1–4 miles with surf practice at the mouth during a rising tide, and a 2-mile introductory coastal tour to Duxbury Reef in waves to 3 feet and wind to 15 knots.

Advanced: 4+ miles with good kayak surfing at the mouth in waves to 6 feet or more and access to coastal touring (see rte. 15).

TRIP DURATION: Part to full day.

NAVIGATION AIDS: USGS: *Bolinas* (7.5 minute) and NOAA chart 18647. Wx radio: "Point Arena to Pigeon Point"; buoys: Point Reyes, S.E. Farallon Island, and Point Bonita.

TIDAL INFORMATION: Extensive mudflats exposed at tide heights below 3 feet; strong currents at mouth during ebb.

CAUTIONS: Mud, wind, tidal currents, and surf at mouth; avoid disturbing sensitive seal haul outs and birding areas. Surly locals.

TRIP PLANNING: Paddle early to avoid wind and during rising tide to avoid getting stuck in the mud. The higher the tide, the more places you can paddle; launching from Highway 1 sites requires 3–4 feet of tide minimum. At lower tides, use the alternate launch site at the mouth of the lagoon and follow the boat channel, which is navigable for a mile or more except during extreme low tides.

LAUNCH SITES: There are several roadside launch sites off Highway 1 where it borders Bolinas Lagoon between Olema and Stinson Beach. The best pullouts are at highway marker 15⁶⁷ just south of the entrance to Audubon Canyon Ranch and 15³² just south of Volunteer Canyon. Look for the small, green signs warning not to disturb the harbor seals. **Alternate launch sites:** To reach the mouth of the lagoon, turn west off Highway 1 to the unsigned Olema-Bolinas Road (xenophobic locals tear down the signs), which follows the lagoon's north shore. Turn left at the T intersection to stay on Olema-Bolinas Road where Horseshoe Hills Road joins it from the north. Follow it through "downtown" Bolinas to a dead end at the lagoon mouth, or turn right onto Brighton Avenue for a surf launch with better parking.

DIRECTIONS

START: Head southwest from **highway marker 15⁶⁷**, following the channel that parallels the road. *Caution:* Watch out for mud and don't disturb the seals hauled out on the mudflats. *Sidetrip:* At high tide you can wander north across the mudflats and marshes at the back of the lagoon.

MILE 0.5: Launch site at **highway marker 15³²**.

MILE 1.25: Channel bends west away from highway and toward the lagoon mouth. *Caution:* There are many seals in this area. *Sidetrip:* At high tide you can continue along the highway and explore the mudflats in the lagoon's southeastern arm.

MILE 2.25: Landing options at either side of **lagoon mouth** or on **Kent Island** at high tide. *Caution:* Ocean-going currents in mouth during ebb tide; waves and surf. Helmets and surf zone experience required beyond the mouth. *Sidetrip:* At high tide you can explore the narrow boat channel that winds around Kent Island and into the salt marsh, retracing your route before the tide turns or completing the clockwise loop back to the launch site at extreme high tide. *Caution:* Don't get caught in the mud by a falling tide.

MILE 4.0: Return to launch site.

OTHER OPTIONS: Ocean paddlers can shred the classic kayak surfing break at the mouth or explore north to Duxbury Reef. *Caution:* The exposed coastline and rock gardens north of the reef recommended for advanced coastal paddlers only.

Bolinas Lagoon & Duxbury Reef

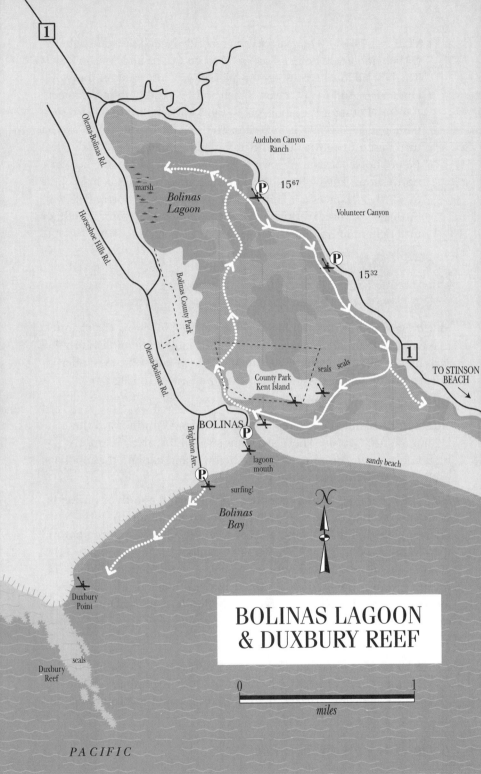

Audubon Canyon Ranch

15^{67}

Volunteer Canyon

15^{32}

marsh

Bolinas Lagoon

Olema-Bolinas Rd.

Horseshoe Hills Rd.

Bolinas County Park

Olema-Bolinas Rd.

County Park
Kent Island

seals   seals

1

TO STINSON
BEACH

BOLINAS

Brighton Ave.

lagoon
mouth

sandy beach

surfing!

*Bolinas
Bay*

N

Duxbury
Point

seals

Duxbury
Reef

BOLINAS LAGOON
& DUXBURY REEF

0   1

miles

PACIFIC

OCEAN

Responsible Paddler's Guide to Bolinas Lagoon

Launch sites along Highway 1 display signs reminding paddlers that Bolinas Lagoon is a sensitive resting and pupping habitat for harbor seals *(Phoca vitulina)*. When resting seals raise their heads to look at you, one sign explains, you are too close and should back off. Frightening seals off their haul outs not only reduces breeding success and increases the likelihood they will abandon the site, it is a federal offense carrying fines up to $10,000. Lagoon birdlife, too, is sensitive. Although shorebirds are fairly tolerant of kayakers, waterfowl are not. Over a dozen species of ducks frequent the lagoon between November and February. Used to being hunted, these skittish ducks are easily spooked by boats and flailing paddles. Not realizing Bolinas is a rare "safe harbor," they may fly off to other areas where hunting is permitted. The locals like their wildlife, so it's important for kayakers not to drive it away if we want to continue paddling this fine lagoon.

Where to Eat & Where to Stay

RESTAURANTS Few choices, but there is good food at good value at the **Bolinas Bay Bakery & Cafe** (415–868–0211) in Bolinas and the **Parkside Cafe** (415–868–1272) in Stinson Beach. **LODGING** One Fifty-Five Pine Bed and Breakfast is located a short walk from the beach in Bolinas (415–868–0263). (See Route 11: Central Tomales for other options.) **CAMPING** There is camping at nearby **Steep Ravine Environmental Camp**, part of the **Golden Gate National Recreation Area** (415–331–1540) or at **Pan Toll State Park Headquarters**, Park Net (800–444–7275). (See also Route 10: North Tomales.)

San Francisco Bay

Route 17:

China Camp

The convoluted shoreline of this 1,500-acre park stretches 3 miles along rocky bluffs backed by rolling hills of thickly forested oak woodland, offering panoramic views of San Pablo Bay and the East Bay hills. This series of points and small coves fringed with salt marsh creates great feeding grounds for the nearby heron and egret rookeries on Marin Islands Reserve, and narrow, winding channels give kayakers access to the marsh at high tide. Essentially undeveloped, the area retains much of the character (as well as several original structures) from the days when it was a Chinese fishing village. For a historical perspective, stop by the small museum near the launch beach.

TRIP HIGHLIGHTS: Flatwater paddling, bird watching, and scenery.

TRIP RATING:

Beginner: 1–5+ miles of flatwater in winds to 10 knots.

Intermediate: 1–10 miles; those with strong open-water skills can paddle out to Marin Islands to explore the egret rookery in winds below 15 knots.

TRIP DURATION: Part to full day.

NAVIGATION AIDS: *China Camp State Park* map, available at visitor center, also describes the area's rich cultural and natural history; NOAA chart 18653. Wx radio: "Wind forecast for San Francisco and San Pablo Bays"; buoys: Point Blunt and Davis Point.

TIDAL INFORMATION: Tides below 2 feet expose broad mudflats near shore.

CAUTIONS: Mud, offshore winds, closed areas, fishing lines, and light boat traffic.

TRIP PLANNING: Paddle early before wind with at least 2 to 3 feet of tide; a rising tide is best.

LAUNCH SITE: From Highway 101 in San Rafael, take North San Pedro Road exit and follow signs to China Camp State Park: head east on North Point San Pedro Road through the park to the beach at China Camp Historic Area. There is a $3.00 day-use fee with snack concession, museum, rest rooms, and picnic area. **Alternate launch sites:** Bullhead Flat, 0.5 mile north of the historic area, has rest rooms and fee as well as an outdoor shower but fewer parking sites and less wind protection; or try McNears Beach County Park, a mile south, $5.00 parking fee or Bucks Launch ($5.00).

DIRECTIONS

START: From the beach at **China Camp Historic Area,** head northwest along the shore. *Sidetrips:* Experienced open-bay paddlers may paddle south around Point San Pedro to explore the egret rookery at Marin Islands bird refuge. *Caution:* This is an open-bay crossing subject to strong offshore winds; no landing permitted on the islands.

MILE 0.25: Tiny **Rat Rock Island**—off the first point—is more picturesque than its name suggests. *Caution:* In spring this can be the nesting site of Canada geese, do not disturb.

MILE 0.75: **Bullhead Flat**, an optional launch site with rest rooms.

MILE 1.0: Beyond the pilings off **Buckeye Point**, the salt marsh begins.

MILE 2.0: Except during extreme high tides, **Jakes Island** looks like a point of land surrounded by the salt marsh. *Sidetrip:* A narrow tidal creek just past Jakes is navigable for 0.5 mile to the northwest edge of **Turtle Back**, where it forks and is wide enough to turn around.

MILE 2.75: The mouth of **Gallinas Creek** and site of **Bucks Launch**, a good spot for a snack and rest. *Sidetrip:* Continue up Gallinas Creek for another 1.5 miles.

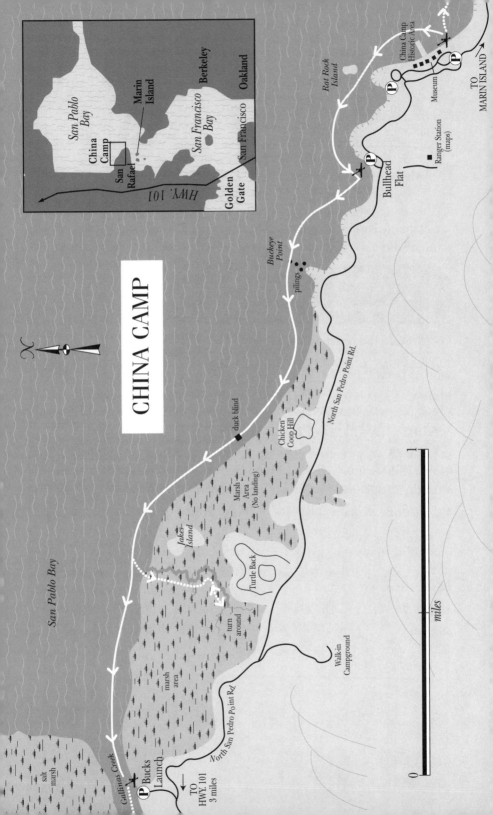

CHINA CAMP

San Pablo Bay

Rat Rock Island

China Camp Historic Area

Museum

P

P

TO MARIN ISLAND

Ranger Station (maps)

P

Bullhead Flat

Buckeye Point

pilings

North San Pedro Point Rd.

duck blind

Chicken Coop Hill

Marsh Area (No landing)

Jakes Island

Turtle Back

Walk-in Campground

turn around

marsh area

salt marsh

Gallinas Creek

P Bucks Launch

TO HWY 101 3 miles

North San Pedro Point Rd.

miles

0

Inset map

San Pablo Bay

Marin Island

Berkeley

Oakland

San Francisco Bay

China Camp

San Rafael

HWY. 101

Golden Gate

San Francisco

History of China Camp

The earliest people known to to be at this site were the Coastal Miwok, relying on food sources provided by the surrounding oak forests, and the bountiful waters of San Pablo Bay. *Californio* ranchers, descendants from the Spanish and other Europeans conquering the American west, displaced the Miwok during the nineteenth century. About the same time, the first Chinese Americans arrived in search of wealth in the West. Drawn by the sustenance of San Pablo Bay and the unoccupied beaches fringing the ranches, some of them developed a shrimp industry at "China Camp," fishing there into the twentieth century. Their buildings, pier, and photos at the visitor interpretive center make an interesting launch site for kayakers at the beginning of the twenty-first century.

Where to Eat & Where to Stay

RESTAURANTS   There are snack bars at **China Camp Historic Area** (415–459–9877) and **Bucks Launch** (415–472–1502) and many restaurants in nearby San Rafael.   **LODGING**   For information about lodging, call San Rafael Chamber of Commerce (415–454–4163). (See Route 18: Richardson Bay and Route 10: North Tomales.)   **CAMPING**   There are walk-in sites at **China Camp Back Ranch Meadows**; make reservations through Park Net (800–444–7275). (See Route 10: North Tomales Bay.)

Route 18:

▬ ▬ ▬ ▬ ▬ ▬ ▬ ▬ ▬ ▬ ▬ ▬ ▬ ➤

Richardson Bay to Angel Island

Richardson Bay offers aspriring intermediates a great introduction to open-bay paddling with all the rewards and challenges of the greater bay—scenery, tidal currents, exposure, boat traffic, fog, and wind—in a more protected setting. Less-experienced kayakers can stay near the shoreline or confine their exploration to the back of the bay, while more experienced paddlers can venture out toward "the Gate" (the Golden Gate Bridge, the waters, and the general vicinity beneath the bridge) or cross Raccoon Strait to Angel Island for a day trip or overnight camping. On the island, climb to the summit of Mount Livermore for excellent views of the bay and the Golden Gate Bridge or visit the museum at the old immigration station, the colonial garrisons, and the Ayala Cove coffee shop.

TRIP HIGHLIGHTS: Views of the Golden Gate Bridge, overnight camping, paddling in tidal currents, and bird watching.

TRIP RATING:

Beginner: 2–5 miles, depending on conditions; stay along shore in Richardson Bay or explore the salt marsh in the back of the bay.

Intermediate: 5–15 miles. For those with previous experience paddling in currents and strong open-water rescue skills, a crossing to Angel Island is possible on days when winds are below 15 knots and tidal currents are weak (or during slack tide). A trip leader with previous local experience is suggested. Yellow Bluff tide rips are an excellent training ground during ebb currents of 1–3 knots.

Advanced: 5–15 miles; same as intermediate trip but in stronger winds and currents; tide rips play in 3–6 knots currents at Yellow Bluff and Raccoon Strait during big ebbs.

TRIP DURATION: Part day, full day, or overnight.

NAVIGATION AIDS: NOAA chart 18649 or 18653. Wx radio: "wind forecast for San Francisco Bay"; buoys: Point Bonita, Golden Gate, and Point Blunt/Angel Island.

TIDAL INFORMATION: Complex tidal flows make San Francisco Bay *the* place to learn about paddling in currents.

CAUTIONS: Boat traffic, strong currents, and nasty tide rips—especially in Raccoon Strait and off Yellow Bluff during ebb tide—strong afternoon winds and heavy fog. Don't cross to Angel Island if you're not comfortable reading tide and current tables or navigating by compass in fog. If planning to circumnavigate Angel Island, expect afternoon winds to cause confused seas and surf along the island's southwest shore—helmets and surf zone experience recommended for landings.

TRIP PLANNING: Paddle early before wind and use tidal currents to your advantage: explore the back-bay marsh on an incoming tide to avoid being stuck in the mud; ride the ebb currents to Yellow Bluff and return on the flood; or cross to Angel Island at slack after a morning ebb and return with the afternoon flood, avoiding peak ebb and the tide rips in Raccoon Strait. Autumn has less fog and wind. Winter and spring runoff creates stronger ebbs.

LAUNCH SITE: Three miles north of the Golden Gate on Highway 101, take the Sausalito/Marin City exit and head south on Bridgeway Boulevard into Sausalito. Turn left on Napa (the first street after the light at Easterby), then take a right into the parking lot at Dunphy Park. The farther into the lot you can park the better because the launch beach is on the far end of the park on the other side of the gazebo. Parking is free and overnight parking is allowed. **Alternate launch sites:** Sea Trek at Schoonmaker Bay has a nicer beach but difficult parking (415–332–4465). From Horseshoe Bay Marina (see rte. 19), advanced paddlers can make the longer crossing to Angel Island during the opposite tide scenario.

DIRECTIONS

START: Head northeast from Dunphy Park toward the boat channel, following the docks on your right.

MILE 0.5: When you reach the channel, bear right and follow it along the docks, staying well to the right or crossing the channel and skirting its left edge to avoid boat traffic. *Sidetrips:* Turn left and follow the shore into the back of the bay at high tide to explore 3 miles or more into the protected marshes.

MILE 1.0: Anywhere along this stretch offers the shortest crossing to the cliffs on **Belvedere Peninsula**. The most conservative and scenic route is toward the middle of the peninsula or the left end (as opposed to the point), checking your drift against the midbay buoys and the far shore. There are no good landing beaches along Belvedere's cliffs, so don't cross unless you are prepared to be in your boat for a while. *Sidetrips:* Instead of crossing to Belvedere, continue along the Sausalito shore for another 2.5 miles to **Yellow Bluff** or follow the shore for another mile to **Horseshoe Cove** for views of the Golden Gate. *Caution:* Strong currents and tide rips occur at Yellow Bluff, especially during ebb tide; expect rougher conditions when approaching the Gate.

MILE 2.0: Follow the cliffs toward **Point Belvedere,** gawking at the amazing homes perched there.

MILE 2.5: Point Belvedere is a good place to reassess conditions for crossing **Raccoon Strait**. *Caution:* Be aware of strong currents that sometimes sweep toward the point from several hundred yards inside Richardson Bay. At the point, tide rips, submerged rocks, and exposure to wind can create challenging conditions. Out in the strait some of the bay's more exciting *or excruciating* tide rips (depending on your abilities) form. If your skills are up to the conditions, cross to Point Stuart on Angel Island, using a ferry angle to compensate for currents.

MILE 3.0: From **Point Stuart** continue northeast along the island toward **Ayala Cove**. *Sidetrips:* Head to the right around Point Stuart for .25 mile to land at the **West Garrison** to stretch or to use the public rest room.

MILE 3.25: A small beach in the middle of the cove gives access to the trail to the two **kayak campsites**.

MILE 4.0: Land in front of the lawn on the right side of **Ayala Cove** to hike, picnic or investigate the coffee shop and museums. Return to Dunphy Park by retracing your route or by crossing Raccoon Strait to Tiburon, following the shore back into Richardson Bay, and retracing your route from there. *Sidetrips:* Continue another mile to a quieter beach at **China Cove** and tour the museum at the old immigration station. Circumnavigators can finish the 4-mile loop back to Point Stuart

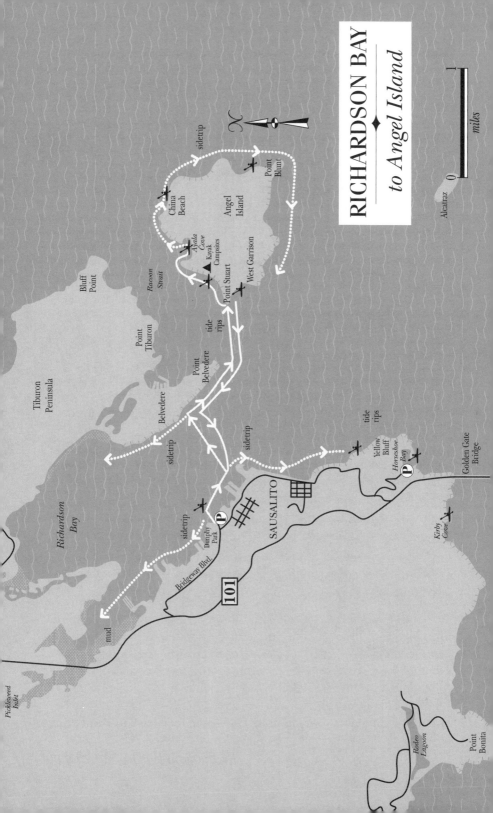

RICHARDSON BAY
to Angel Island

miles

Alcatraz

sidetrip

China Beach

Point Blunt

Angel Island

Ayala Cove

Kayak Campsites

West Garrison

Point Stuart

Racoon Strait

Bluff Point

Point Tiburon

tide rips

Point Belvedere

Tiburon Peninsula

Belvedere

sidetrip

sidetrip

sidetrip

Richardson Bay

sidetrip

tide rips

Yellow Bluff

Horseshoe Bay

Dunphy Park

Bridgeway Blvd.

SAUSALITO

Kirby Cove

Golden Gate Bridge

101

mud

Pickleweed Inlet

Rodeo Lagoon

Point Bonita

and retrace their route back to Dunphy. *Caution:* Westerly winds funneling through the Gate onto Point Blunt are consistently recorded as among the strongest in the bay, often causing confused seas to batter the cliffs between Points Blunt and Stuart.

Where to Eat & Where to Stay

RESTAURANTS Among Sausalito's many choices is **Margaritaville** (415–331–3226) south of Dunphy Park. **LODGING** Reservations required well in advance at **Holiday Inn Express** on the water in the back of Richardson Bay (800–258–3894) or across the street at either the **Fireside Motel** (415–332–6906) or **Fountain Motel** (415–332–1732). **CAMPING** Check with rangers on Angel Island at 415–435–5390 to reserve the two kayak campsites well ahead of time. (Eventually these sites may be included with the island's other campsites, which can be reserved through Park Net at 800–444–7275.) See Route 19: Golden Gate for more options.

China Cove & the Old Immigration Station

An interesting slice of Angel Island history occurred during the early portion of the twentieth century when the island served as the West Coast's version of Ellis Island. Immigrants landing in California at that time came primarily from China, and their detainment allowed customs inspectors time to assess the newcomers' paperwork and health. You can visit the holding dormitories and the guided tour is highly recommended. The guides will share accounts of the people held there, honoring the courage and strength of those who risked venturing to America.

Route 19:

━━ ━━ ━━ ━━ ━━ ━━ ━━ ━━ ━━ ━━ ━━ ━━ ━━ ━━ ➤

Golden Gate to Point Bonita & Beyond

From the seat of a kayak, the enormous scale of the scenery as you paddle out beneath the Golden Gate—the bridge towering 200 feet above your head, the 600-foot cliffs of the Marin Headlands, and perhaps the skyscraper hull of a passing supertanker—can overwhelm. But you'll need to pay attention to the water. Twice a day all of San Francisco, Suisuin, and San Pablo Bays (as well as some 80 percent of the state's freshwater runoff from the Sacramento River and several Sierra Mountain rivers) funnels out through the barely mile-wide gap beneath the bridge; and twice each day the Pacific floods back in, creating the strongest, most challenging tidal currents in California. During peak flows, currents faster than you can paddle, sometimes in excess of 6 knots, can sweep you away with them. Understanding the complexities of the tides—how to hitch a ride on these powerful liquid conveyer belts *and how to pick a time and a day to avoid them*—are essential skills for the well-rounded kayaker. For those ready to bump their skills up a notch, the waters of the Gate are the master teacher. Beyond the Gate to Point Bonita, several fairly protected beaches make good lunch stops, and the cliffy open-coast vista beyond the point is spectacular.

TRIP HIGHLIGHTS: Awesome views of the Golden Gate Bridge and Marin Headlands; state's premier spot for learning about tidal currents.

TRIP RATING:

> *Beginner:* 1-mile, open-bay crossing as far as the Gate not recommended unless led by experienced paddler on a calm day during a weak flood tide.

> *Intermediate:* 4-mile round-trip to Point Diablo, 6-miles to Bonita Cove. Going beyond the Gate not recommended without previous experience paddling in currents and strong open-water skills; ability to read local current guides a must; experience navigating in fog and a trip leader with previous local experience suggested.

> *Advanced:* The 7-mile round-trip to Point Bonita, with another 2 miles of extreme open coast to Rodeo Beach, recommended in seas below 6 feet, winds below 20 knots; features tide rips with surfable standing waves, arches, and rock gardens.

TRIP DURATION: Part to full day.

NAVIGATION AIDS: NOAA chart 18649. Wx radio: "Wind forecast for San Francisco Bay"; buoys: Point Bonita, Golden Gate, and Point Blunt/Angel Island.

TIDAL INFORMATION: The swiftest currents in the state flow through the Golden Gate.

CAUTIONS: Strong currents and tide rips. Small Craft Advisories for winds above 20 knots are typical most spring and summer

Golden Gate to Point Bonita & Beyond

afternoons. The bay is (in)famous for fog. Don't paddle here unless you are comfortable navigating by compass. Boat traffic of every description: The bay is one of the world's major commercial and recreational ports. Avoid crossing shipping lanes, freighters move deceptively fast and can't stop.

TRIP PLANNING: Ride the ebb on your way out and use the flood on your way back. Unless you're looking for excitement, pick a day with currents less than 3 knots or so, and/or avoid the Gate during times of maximum current. Check your weather radio throughout the day; expect strong westerlies in the 20-knot range to funnel through the Gate. Hug the shore to minimize effects of wind, current, fog, and boat traffic. The best places for tide rips play are Yellow Bluff on the ebb and North Tower on the flood.

LAUNCH SITE: To reach Horseshoe Bay Marina from Highway 101, exit on Alexander Avenue (just north of the bridge) and head downhill about 0.25 mile toward Sausalito. Take the first left. Take the first right (sort of a U turn) and keep heading downhill toward the water and Fort Baker. At the bottom of the hill, take a right at the stop sign and keep heading toward the water. Take the second left and look for the boat ramp at Horseshoe Bay Marina in front of the Coast Guard Station. There is free parking to the left of the launch ramp. **Alternate launch site:** Dunphy Park in Sausalito (see Route 18: Richardson Bay).

DIRECTIONS

START: Leaving **Horseshoe Bay**, turn right, rounding the pier well beyond fishing lines, and follow the cliffs. *Sidetrip:* Turn left and follow the shore to Yellow Bluff for more protection or to play in the tide rips during an ebb.

MILE 0.5: The lee of **Lime Point** beneath the unmistakable **Golden Gate Bridge** provides a great photo op and a good place to reassess conditions. *Caution:* On rough days conditions immediately worsen on rounding Lime Point: Wind, ocean swell, and current can create confused seas. Swing wide to avoid washing into the cliffs. Avoid this area during strong ebbs when currents faster than you can paddle against sweep seaward.

Golden Gate to Point Bonita & Beyond

MILE 1.5: **Kirby Cove**, the long beach on your right with a staircase on its far end, makes a good place for a break. It is one of the few beaches in the area protected from prevailing swell and winds, and it has pit toilets hidden in the trees. *Caution:* Surf looks nonexistent, but it often dumps quick and hard on this beach. Far left side is more protected; helmets are recommended.

MILE 2.0: **Point Diablo**, the distinct point with the navigational horn, is where conditions generally get rougher still, so it's a good turnaround on many days.

MILE 2.5: Several scenic pocket beaches dot **Bonita Cove**. *Caution:* Steep beaches make for challenging landings in all but the smallest swell.

MILE 3.5: Point Bonita makes a good turn-around spot for all but advanced open-coast kayakers. Routinely battered by waves and strong winds, the steep cliffs beyond the point are as exposed as they are dramatic. *Sidetrips:* Depending on conditions, experts may find the rock gardens and arches from the point onward extremely challenging and beautiful—or extremely hazardous.

MILE 4.5: A sandy but exposed beach at **Rodeo Beach** offers the only landing spot on this stretch of cliffs, but when surf is above 6 feet, it's recommended for experts only.

OTHER OPTIONS: Advanced coastal paddlers can run a shuttle and enter the Gate from several points to the north. This section of coast is extremely scenic and extremely exposed, with towering cliffs and few beaches besides the launch sites listed here north to south: Stinson Beach (10 miles to Point Bonita), Muir Beach (4.5 miles), and Rodeo Beach (1 mile). All beaches can be reached from Highway 1.

Where to Eat & Where to Stay

RESTAURANTS AND LODGING (See Route 18: Richardson Bay.) **CAMPING** From April through October there are walk-in sites available at **Kirby Cove**, and others are available at **Rob Hill** through **Golden Gate National Recreation Area** (415–561–4304). Also nearby is **China Camp State Park** (415–456–0766) also with walk-in sites.

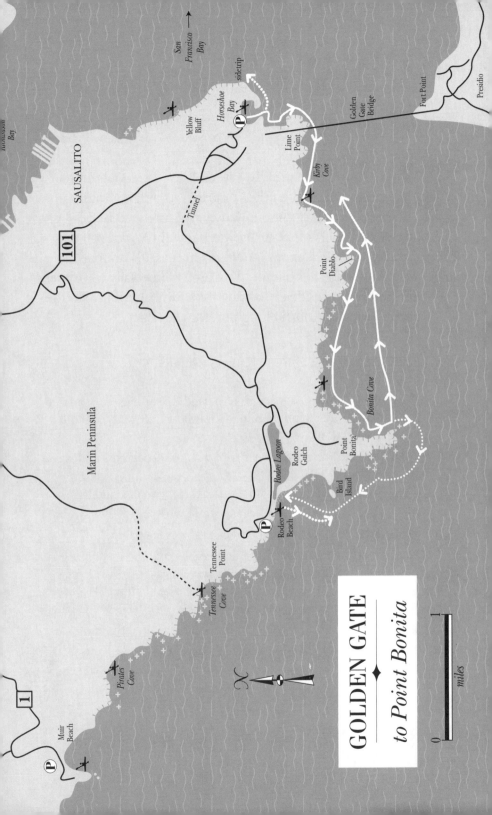

San Francisco Bay

Tiburon Bay

SAUSALITO

Marin Peninsula

101

Tunnel

Yellow Bluff

Horseshoe Bay

sidetrip

P

Lime Point

Kirby Cove

Golden Gate Bridge

Fort Point

Presidio

Point Diablo

Bonita Cove

Rodeo Lagoon

Rodeo Gulch

Point Bonita

Bird Island

P

Rodeo Beach

Tennessee Point

Tennessee Cove

Pirates Cove

Muir Beach

1

P

GOLDEN GATE

◆

to Point Bonita

0   1

miles

Route 20:

Bair Island Reserve & Corkscrew Slough

Bair Island Ecological Reserve, a 1,600-acre tidal marsh tucked away at the edges of urban sprawl, is a wilderness for the myopic: surrounded by city, traversed by power lines, but chockablock with shorebirds. And once you slip into its maze of narrow, winding channels, it's not hard to lose oneself in the solitude. This area is especially convenient for South Bay residents looking for a local alternative to the long drive to Elkhorn Slough or Tomales Bay.

TRIP HIGHLIGHTS: Good birding, solitude.

TRIP RATING:

Beginner: 1–7 miles or more of protected exploration for paddlers with a basic understanding of tides and boat traffic and a good sense of direction.

Intermediate: Longer flatwater trips with some currents and access to open bay.

TRIP DURATION: Part to full day.

NAVIGATION AIDS: USGS *Redwood Point* (7.5 minute) and NOAA chart 18651. Wx radio: "Wind forecast for San Francisco Bay."

TIDAL INFORMATION: Although much paddling is still possible at low tide, you'll need 2–3 feet of tide height to get through Corkscrew Slough and to explore smaller side channels. Expect moderate currents in constricted channels during big tide changes.

CAUTIONS: Winds, boat traffic in harbor, currents, and mud.

TRIP PLANNING: Choose a high, rising tide and give yourself plenty of time.

LAUNCH SITE: To reach the Redwood City Marina Boat Ramp, take Highway 101 to the Seaport Boulevard exit (at Highway 84 junction) and follow signs to the Port of Redwood City, turning left on Chesapeake Street to where it ends at the boat ramp.There is a $3.50 launch fee, but parking is free.

DIRECTIONS

START: Launch from dock or boat ramp and follow the right shore northeast toward the bay. Note the large, white mountain of salt on your left: This landmark can be seen from many places in the slough and will help you keep your bearings.

MILE 1.5: Turn left into **Corkscrew Slough** at the red #14 channel marker, checking the location of the salt mountain as you do. *Sidetrip:* You can also paddle several miles into Westpoint Slough on the right side of the channel if you're looking to try someplace new.

MILE 2.0: First channel on the right offers sidetrip possibilities (but it is noted here to distinguish it from the next channel).

MILE 2.2: The second channel on your right **(GPS: W 122° 12' 37", N 37° 31' 42")**, the narrow, "secret passage" through the heart of the **Bair Island Ecological Reserve** is the scenic route to San Francisco Bay. It's smaller than the first channel you just passed, with small, mud mounds that partially block the entrance. Turn right into the channel and take the left fork, which runs parallel to Corkscrew Slough. *Sidetrip:* You can also continue through the deeper Corkscrew Slough if you want more mileage: The counterclockwise loop through Corkscrew and Steinberger Sloughs to Smith Slough and back to the marina is 9 miles; the clockwise trip around Bair Island is 11.

MILE 2.3: Stay right from here on. Follow the **first channel on your right** toward the power lines, staying right at the fork and keeping to the deeper right-hand side of the channel.

MILE 2.4: Take the next channel on your right and paddle under both the power lines and the small, wooden boardwalk. From here it's a straight shot along the levee to the bay. *Sidetrip:* Some smaller channels on your left are navigable if you're in the mood to explore dead ends.

Bair Island Reserve & Corkscrew Slough

MILE 3.2: Views of **San Francisco Bay** and the East Bay hills open up at the edge of Bair Island, as does exposure to the wind. On windy days you may want to retrace your path; otherwise continue clockwise around the island. *Sidetrip:* A maze of channels angles back into Bair Island on your left (bearing 220° MN) for those who enjoy meandering (and have a good sense of direction). For a workout take the long way home down Steinberger Slough and return via either the more scenic Corkscrew or the shorter Smith Slough.

MILE 3.6: At higher tides **shell beaches** along this stretch offer mud-free landings for a lunch break. *Caution:* Although not technically permitted, refuge managers won't begrudge your landing if you stay near your kayak, don't walk around in the sensitive marshlands, and don't disturb the feeding birds.

MILE 4.4: Turn right at **channel marker #8** at **Redwood Point**, which is the last shell beach and the most accessible at lower tides.

MILE 5.2: Cross under power lines at the mouth of Corkscrew Slough, looking for egret nests on the towers, to complete your loop around Bair Island.

MILE 6.8: Return to the marina.

Where to Eat & Where to Stay

RESTAURANTS There are no restaurants in the immediate area. Follow Seaport Boulevard under Highway 101 into Redwood City for a selection of fast-food chains. **LODGING AND CAMPING** Not exactly a "destination" location, the light industrial area offers no lodging nearby. (See Route 19: Golden Gate.)

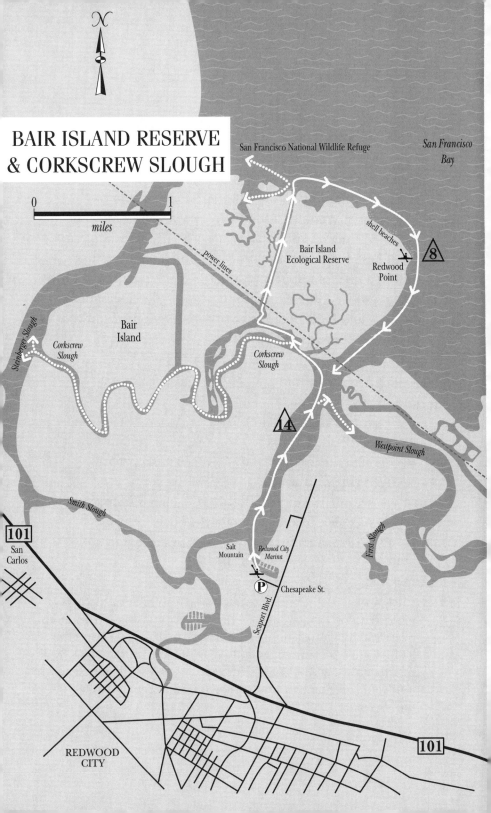

BAIR ISLAND RESERVE & CORKSCREW SLOUGH

San Francisco National Wildlife Refuge

San Francisco Bay

0 — 1
miles

power lines

Bair Island Ecological Reserve

shell beaches

△8

Redwood Point

Steinberger Slough

Bair Island

Corkscrew Slough

Corkscrew Slough

△14

Westpoint Slough

Smith Slough

First Slough

101
San Carlos

Salt Mountain

Redwood City Marina

Ⓟ Chesapeake St.

Seaport Blvd.

REDWOOD CITY

101

Route 21:

![arrow with dashes]

Newark Slough Wildlife Refuge

The Newark Slough's narrow channel meanders through the salt marsh of Don Edwards San Francisco Bay National Wildlife Refuge, the nation's largest urban wildlife refuge at 20,000 acres. Particularly convenient for both East and South Bay residents, this launch site lies within a mile of refuge headquarters and its extensive visitor center, with its fine exhibits interpreting the fascinating ecology and biology of the marshlands and the hundreds of wildlife species residing there.

TRIP HIGHLIGHTS: Good birding, peaceful marsh.

TRIP RATING:

Beginner: 1–7+ miles of narrow protected waterway, easy paddling in winds to 10 or 15 knots.

Intermediate/Advanced: 7+ miles with access to open bay.

TRIP DURATION: Part day.

NAVIGATION AIDS: USGS: *Newark* (7.5 minute) and NOAA chart 18651. Wx radio: "Wind forecast for San Francisco Bay."

TIDAL INFORMATION: Tidal currents and mud can cause problems during low and falling tides.

CAUTIONS: Mud, currents, and afternoon winds.

TRIP PLANNING: Check tides and launch an hour or two before high tide (don't forget to make the correction). Very muddy at low tides. With no good landing sites in the marsh, paddle out only half as far as you want to go without getting out of your kayak to rest, then turn around and head back. Paddle early before the wind and make time to see the refuge's visitor center exhibits in the afternoon.

NEWARK SLOUGH
WILDLIFE REFUGE

RED HILL
▲ 285

Don Edwards
San Francisco Bay National Wildlife Refuge

0   1
miles

N

■cabins
Visitor
Center
foot
bridge
foot
bridge

P

Paseo Padre Pkwy.
Hwy. 84
Thornton Ave.
Marshlands Rd.

Dunbarton Bridge/Hwy. 84

Newark Slough

Salt
Pond

Hetch Hetchy Aqueduct

SAN FRANCISCO BAY

Salt
Pond

drawbridge

Plummer Creek

Dunbarton
Bridge

Southern Pacific Railroad

Dunbarton Point

SAN FRANCISCO

BAY

LAUNCH SITE: To reach Newark Slough Boat Launch, from Highway 84 take Thornton Road south (the Paseo Padre exit if you're heading west on 84) and turn right on Marshlands Road. The boat ramp is in the parking lot at this corner. No fees or facilities.

DIRECTIONS

START: Head right after launching, meandering along the bends in the channel. *Sidetrip:* Shallow marshlands on right can be explored at high tide.

MILE 1.0: Pass under a **footbridge** as you follow a straightaway that parallels the main hiking trail from the visitor center.

MILE 1.25: After a second footbridge, pass the **historic cabins** on the right just before the channel bends hard left.

MILE 2.25: Slough nears **Dunbarton Bridge** before curving left and heading back into the marsh. *Caution:* If continuing beyond here, expect the wind to be in your face on the return.

MILE 3.5: The **Hetch Hetchy Aqueduct** is probably a good place to turn around or risk running out of tide. *Sidetrip:* If you are intent on pushing the tide/mud envelope, it's possible to continue and explore various side channels, Plummer Creek, or the open bay beyond. *Caution:* The farther you go, the more you'll risk losing your way in the fog or getting stuck in the mud.

Where to Eat & Where to Stay

RESTAURANTS AND LODGING Not exactly a "destination" spot; various chain restaurants and lodging are available in Newark and the surrounding East Bay sprawl. **CAMPING** There are no camping facilities nearby. (See Route 24: Pillar Point Harbor and Beyond.)

Location of Route Goes Here

Monterey Bay
National Marine
Sanctuary & Vicinity

Route 22:

━━ ━━ ━━ ━━ ━ ━ ━ ━ ━ ━ ━ ━ ➤

Lexington Reservoir

Cradled in the foothills of the Santa Cruz Mountains overlooking the Santa Clara Valley, Lexington Reservoir is especially convenient for South Bay residents seeking a quick getaway and a change of scenery. Although the lake may not quite match our local coastline for dramatic vistas (but then few places can), it nonetheless displays an interesting tapestry of habitats. The lake's steep shores sport a fascinating blend of "ecotones"—areas of overlapping habitat, rich in diversity and sharing the flora and fauna of each. The coastal-scrub chaparral, which dominates the drier, south-facing slopes, blends into areas of oak woodland and mixed-evergreen and riparian forests that are laced with strands of redwood forest in shady canyons and on north-facing slopes. No swimming or gas motors are allowed at this popular fishing lake, so it is a fairly peaceful place to paddle.

TRIP HIGHLIGHTS: Mountain scenery, calm water, and fishing.

TRIP RATING:
Beginner: 1–5 miles of flatwater in winds of 10 to 15 knots.

TRIP DURATION: Part to full day.

NAVIGATION AIDS: A free Lexington Reservoir map is available at lake. Wx radio: "San Jose and South Bay forecast."

TIDAL INFORMATION: Seasonal fluctuations due to rain and water usage; check *San Jose Mercury News* weather section for level updates during summer.

CAUTIONS: Afternoon winds and fishing lines.

TRIP PLANNING: Unfortunately both put ins are at the lake's northern end, meaning that return to the launch site will be into the wind most afternoons. Paddle early to avoid wind or pick a day when the weather forecast is for winds below 15 knots.

LAUNCH SITES: Boat ramp near Lexington Dam can be reached from Santa Clara Valley by taking Bear Creek Road off of Highway 17 (southbound), crossing over the highway and reentering it (northbound), and then exiting on Alma Bridge Road. (From Santa Cruz simply exit on Alma Bridge Road.) After crossing the dam, look for the boat ramp on the right. There is a $3.00 use fee per boat; outhouses. **Alternate launch site:** The shoreline at **Miller Point picnic area,** a bit farther down Alma Bridge Road, has a longer carry but no launch ramp (or associated bottleneck of boats).

DIRECTIONS

START: After launching head left down the lake.

MILE 0.25: **Limekiln Gulch,** the narrow side canyon on the left, makes an interesting sidetrip. At high water you can paddle 0.5 mile, passing through a tunnel beneath the road, to where Limekiln Creek meets the lake.

MILE 0.5: The alternate launch site at **Miller Point picnic area** also makes a good rest stop: The shoreline here is not as steep as other parts of the lake, so it's easier to land, and it has outhouses.

MILE 1.0: **Soda Springs Creek,** the second narrow side canyon, is our favorite sidetrip; it winds over 0.5 mile at high water, through a tunnel, to a nice landing spot along the shady creek bed.

MILE 2.25: Becoming shallower and narrower, the reservoir ends in the willow thickets of **Los Gatos Creek.**

Where to Eat & Where to Stay

RESTAURANTS AND LODGING There is nothing at the lake, but there are many choices in nearby Los Gatos; to get there head west on Highway 9 exit. **CAMPING** None at lake. (See Route 23: Loch Lomond.)

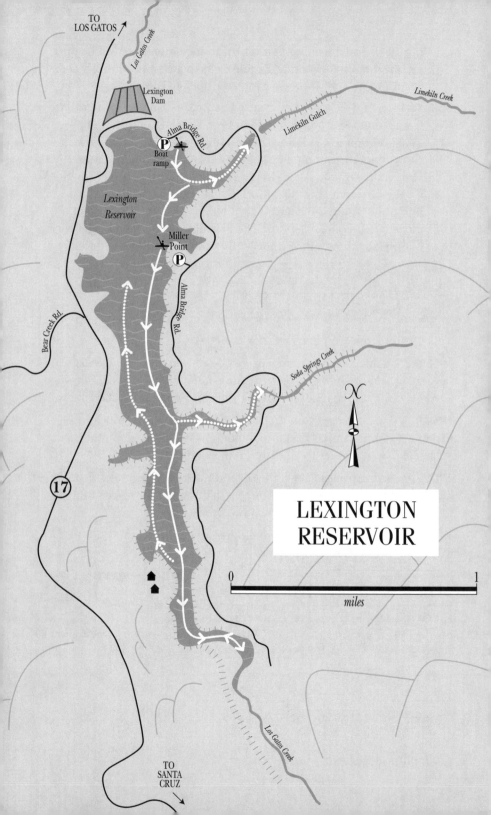

Route 23:

Loch Lomond

Tucked away in a steep fold of the Santa Cruz Mountains, Loch Lomond reservoir, courtesy of the Santa Cruz City Water District, provides a unique opportunity for Central Coast kayakers: paddling through a redwood forest reminiscent of those along the North Coast rivers described earlier. Although quite small, barely 2.5 miles long by 0.5 mile at its widest point, Loch Lomond has much to offer. Along with fine mountain scenery are many nooks to explore, especially the upper reaches of Newell Creek where the moss-covered banks gradually steepen and narrow to less than a boat length, until, ducking under redwood boughs, you reach a dead end. Hiking is good, and it's also a good place to try fishing from your kayak (besides bass and bluegill, the lake is stocked regularly with trout); because gas motors are prohibited, other fishing boats will be quiet ones. Despite the calm water, however, no rolling or rescue practice is allowed because this is a drinking-water supply.

TRIP HIGHLIGHTS: Flatwater, solitude, redwood forest scenery, hiking, and fishing.

TRIP RATING:
Beginner: 1–5 miles of well-protected water.

TRIP DURATION: Part to full day.

NAVIGATION AIDS: Loch Lomond Recreation Area map, available free at park, also describes natural history and boating regulations. Wx radio: "Monterey Bay Area forecast."

TIDAL INFORMATION: Not applicable, but water levels do drop 10 to 20 feet each summer as Santa Cruz slakes its thirst.

CAUTIONS: Lake is open March 1 through September 15 only. Boats need to be off the water approximately one hour before sunset. No swimming, wading, or sailing, and landings permitted only at the three docks. Afternoon wind blowing up canyon from the dam can make return from Newell Creek a slog, especially the last half mile. Watch for poison oak if you go hiking.

TRIP PLANNING: Paddle early morning and late afternoon: There's less wind, and midday during summer can *bake*. No fees charged after 4:00 P.M., so for a free but short trip wait until after collection time, paddle with wind to end of lake, wait for wind to drop, and return before sunset. If returning against the wind, stay close to shore, using points of land as windbreaks. Although it can get more crowded on summer weekends, *crowded* is a relative term here. Still, midweek is especially peaceful.

LAUNCH SITE: From Highway 17 in Scotts Valley, take Mount Hermon Road west toward Felton, turn left on Graham Hill Road, then left again on East Zayante (completing a loop), following signs to Loch Lomond Recreation Area. Go left on Lompico Road, left on West, and right onto Sequoia Drive. There is a $4.00 parking fee plus $2.00 per kayak. Rest rooms and water are available.

DIRECTIONS

START: Head right from the launch ramp off Sequoia Drive. *Sidetrip:* Paddle left toward spillway for a 1-mile round-trip into Buchanan Cove. *Caution:* No boats allowed beyond spillway buoys.

MILE 0.25: One of the lake's two landing docks (besides the launch ramp) is on the far left end of the small island at **Clar Innis Picnic Area**, which may become a peninsula by July as water levels drop.

MILE 0.5: As you round a point on the left at **Bass Cove**, the lake narrows and any tailwind should begin to slacken.

MILE 1.0: The lake's other landing dock at **Deer Flat**, a picnic area with an outhouse, makes a good rest stop. *Sidetrips:* At high water you can explore 0.5 mile or more up **Newell Creek**, the lake's source, a definite highlight of paddling here. The sidetrip up **MacFarlane Cove** is similar but shorter, with interesting remnants of a logging railroad hidden beneath the moss.

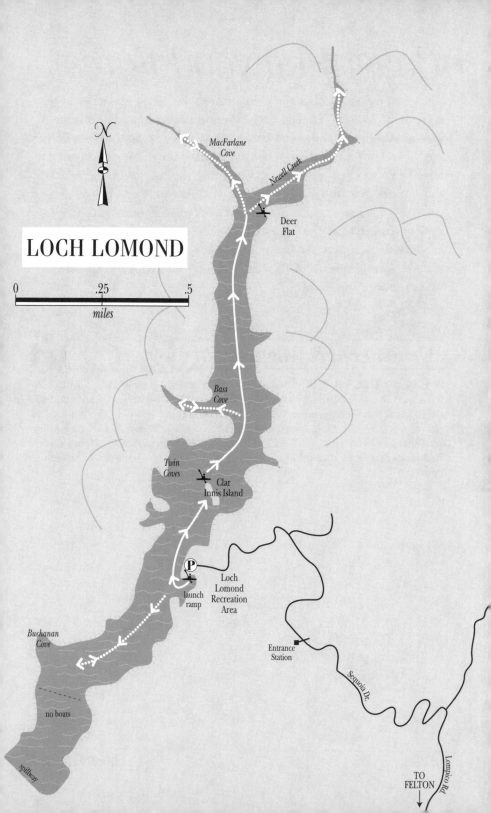

Coast Redwood Forest

The coast redwood, *Sequoia sempervirens*, is the world's tallest tree, growing up to 300 feet. The forest around Loch Lomond, however, was heavily logged at the end of the last century, so all the trees here are second growth. Although not so good for the redwoods, logging allowed a variety of other trees to establish themselves along the lake shore, including Douglas fir, tanbark oak, madrone, and live oak, creating a diverse woodland habitat. Given enough time, and no further disturbance, the "climax forest" of redwoods will eventually reestablish itself over the current "transitional forest." Beneath the canopy, several species of fern thrive, along with redwood sorrel and other shade-loving plants.

Where to Eat & Where to Stay

RESTAURANTS   Sodas and snacks available at the **Park Store** (831–335-7424) beside the launch ramp. **Don Quixote** (831–335-2800) restaurant and bar on Highway 9 in Felton serves Mexican food, steaks, and seafood. There are other restaurants in Felton, Scotts Valley, and Santa Cruz.   **LODGING**   (See Route 26: Santa Cruz Harbor.)   **CAMPING**   Make reservations for **Henry Cowell Redwoods State Park** through Park Net (800–444–7275). (Or see Route 27: Pleasure Point.)

Route 24:

━━ ━ ━ ━ ━ ━ ━ ━ ━ ━ ━ ━ ━ ➤

Pillar Point Harbor & Beyond

Set against a backdrop of coastal mountains and the Pillar Point headlands, this picturesque harbor makes an excellent destination for beginners and experts alike. Within the protection of the breakwater is a 3-mile loop tour with several sandy beaches good for practicing rescues and fine tuning basic skills. Beyond the harbor intermediates can access a semisheltered beach for surf zone practice, while advanced paddlers are within 1 mile of some of the better surfing and rock garden paddling, as well as some of the roughest coastline, in California. This is the Tsunami Rangers' backyard, and several segments from their recent video were filmed nearby. Outside the harbor is also the realm of Mavericks surf break (see "'Monster' Mavericks" on page 131), in winter, one of the biggest waves in the Pacific. The harbor is also the end point for one of the area's classic coastal day trips: the 10-mile, one-way stretch below the towering cliffs of the infamous Devil's Slide (see Other Options on page 132).

TRIP HIGHLIGHTS: Good flat-water touring and excellent access to surfing and open coast.

TRIP RATING:

Beginner: 1–3 mile flat-water loop around harbor in winds 10–15 knots.

Intermediate: 3–mile round-trip for surf zone practice in waves to 3 feet, winds below 15 knots.

Advanced: 2–10+ miles of exposed coast, rock gardens, and surfing.

TRIP DURATION: Part to full day.

NAVIGATION AIDS: USGS *Montara Mountain and Half Moon Bay* (7.5 minute) and NOAA chart 18682. Wx radio: "Point Arena to Pigeon Point"; buoys: Pillar Point.

TIDAL INFORMATION: Little effect except more beach for landing at lower tide.

CAUTIONS: Boat traffic in harbor; wind blowing out toward harbor mouth can make return difficult. Standard coastal hazards beyond the harbor: sneaker waves, submerged rocks, and fog. Be aware that paddling too close to the rocks off Pillar Point has cost one paddler his life (see Monster Mavericks).

TRIP PLANNING: Calmest paddling usually in the mornings although it can be very foggy.

LAUNCH SITE: From Highway 1 in El Granada (just north of Half Moon Bay) turn west into Pillar Point Harbor at the light on Capistrano Road. Go left at Prospect Way, left again on Broadway, and right onto Princeton Avenue. Follow Princeton for several blocks and turn right on Vassar Street into the dirt lot beside the yacht club (or one block farther at the end of West Point Avenue). Parking is free, but there are no facilities. **Alternate launch sites:** near Surfers Beach or at the beach near the boat ramp.

Pillar Point Harbor & Beyond

"Monster" Mavericks & Kevin's Last Wave

For years Mavericks, the surf break off Pillar Point that only breaks under the largest winter swells, was known only by a handful of Nor Cal locals who surfed there, and their tales of Hawaii-sized surf on the California coast were largely ignored, as were their "laughable" claims of it being possibly the world's largest, surfable wave. In the winter of '95–'96, however, when well-known Hawaiian big-wave surfer Mark Foo drowned there, the surfing world stopped laughing and took notice. These days Mavericks pops up routinely in the same sentence with Waimea, Sunset, and Todos Santos and is respected as being among the more treacherous breaks on the planet. Even when Mavericks isn't going off, the coastline here can be treacherous, as kayaker Kevin Anderson discovered too late. According to an accident report in *Sea Kayaker* magazine ("Farewell to Kevin," October 1995), Kevin and a friend were kayak surfing at Microwave, inside the reef from Mavericks, when an especially large set caught the friend and knocked him off his boat. He struggled the quarter mile to shore. As he gathered himself on the beach, he saw no sign of Kevin. Apparently Kevin had attempted to paddle around the reef but did not swing wide enough, and a sneaker wave caught him and slammed him unconscious against the rocks, where he drowned. This danger is not limited to Pillar Point. Virtually any exposed coast area where waves meet rocks has the same potential. Paddlers who lack the experience or alertness to avoid sneaker waves are well advised to explore the open coast with some more wary advanced level companions. California's rocky shores can be a beautiful, exhilarating, wild place to paddle, but to be investigated safely, they demand the appropriate mix of respect, caution, and skill.

START: Head left from the **Princeton Fishing Pier**, contouring along the shore toward the marina jetty. *Sidetrips:* Head out the harbor toward Surfers Beach or portage the sandspit at Pillar Point (see below).

MILE 0.5: At **entrance to inner harbor/marina**, follow jetty around to left for a 0.5-mile loop behind the boat docks, underneath the gangplanks, and out the other side. *Caution:* Watch for traffic, ceding right of way to larger vessels in the narrow channels.

MILE 1.25: Beyond the boat launch at the far side of the harbor is **El Granada Beach**, a good rest stop with rest rooms. *Caution:* There is boat traffic in front of launch ramp. If the wind has come up, this is a good place to turn around and retrace your route, using the inner harbor jetties as windbreaks; if you continue, returning from the main harbor entrance against winds above 10 or 15 knots can be difficult.

MILE 2.0: **Harbor mouth.** *Caution:* Boat traffic; wind exposure.

MILE 2.5: The shallow, sandy beach against the cliffs at **Pillar Point** has the best protection from northwest winds in the harbor, making it a good place to practice skills and a prime lunch spot. Cross the sandspit at the end of the jetty (or scramble up the steep hillside) for views of the reef in front of Mavericks and the wild, open sea beyond. *Sidetrips:* Experienced paddlers can portage the sandspit for access to the open coast (see Other Options).

MILE 3.0: Return to launch beach beside **fishing pier**.

OTHER OPTIONS: Intermediates can paddle out harbor mouth 1.5 miles for surf zone practice at the beach just south of **Surfers Beach** where the bluffs start. (Parking/launching available here for those who just want to surf.) *Caution:* Stay well away from swimmers and surfers at Surfers Beach, but don't go too far south: The beach gets steeper and rougher farther down. For beginners and intermediates we don't recommend practicing here in waves above 3 feet or at high tide. Scout the waves from shore first, don't just paddle out of the harbor and assume you can land safely. A second calm day option for intermediates *with previous coastal paddling experience* or with an advanced paddler leading is to portage the sandspit at Pillar Point for a 1-mile tour along the outside of the breakwater and back in the harbor mouth. *Caution:* Stay close to the

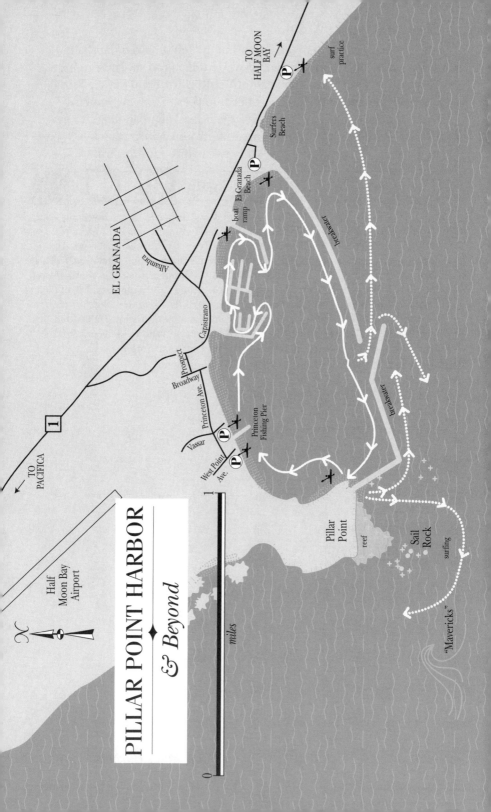

PILLAR POINT HARBOR

& Beyond

0 1 miles

Half Moon Bay Airport

TO PACIFICA

EL GRANADA

Alhambra

Capistrano

Prospect

Broadway

Princeton Ave.

Vassar

West Point Ave.

boat ramp

El Granada Beach

Surfers Beach

TO HALF MOON BAY

surf practice

breakwater

breakwater

Princeton Fishing Pier

Pillar Point

reef

Sail Rock

surfing

"Mavericks"

jetty, especially where it bends sharply to the left, to avoid the shallow reefy area beyond. Experienced coastal paddlers can surf nice rights at "Microwave," a reef break just east of Sail Rock (the square, shed-sized rock near the end of the reef), or head up the coast 3 miles toward Fitzgerald Marine Reserve for excellent rock-garden paddling. A more ambitious option is the 10-mile run down from Pacifica State Beach past Devil's Slide. *Caution:* Advanced skills are required for this trip.

Where to Eat & Where to Stay

RESTAURANTS   Several seafood and fish and chip choices in Pillar Point Harbor, and **Barbara's Fish Trap** (650–728–7049) on Capistrano has a take-out window, convenient for sandy kayakers. For gourmet sandwiches, baked goods, and coffee, head straight across Highway 1, where Capistrano becomes Alhambra, to **Cafe Classique** (650–726–9775).   **LODGING**   **Montara American Youth Hostel** (650–728–7177) has inexpensive lodgings in a converted lighthouse just north of Pillar Point. For fancier digs try **Pillar Point Inn** (650–728–7377) on the waterfront in the harbor.   **CAMPING**   Beach front camping is permitted at **Half Moon Bay State Beach**. Call Park Net (800–444–7275) for reservations. Self-contained RV camping is available on first-come basis in the parking lot at Surfers Beach.

Route 25:

━ ━ ━ ━ ━ ━ ━ ━ ━ ━ ━ ━ ━ ━ ━ ━ ➤

Pigeon Point to Franklin Point Rock Gardens

At first glance there is little to set this 5–mile stretch apart from the other 60 miles of wild open coast between Santa Cruz and San Francisco. Cliffy and scenic, it makes a fine coastal tour, but that's nothing unique here. That two of the area's prominent points were named after ships wrecked on them—the *Carrier Pigeon* and the *Sir John Franklin*—gives a clue (since the first Spanish mariners, this jagged piece of coast has had a reputation for destruction). But on calm days, the same offshore rocks and low reefs that played such hell with early navigators form a playground for experienced paddlers. In the last mile below Franklin Point, a patchy barrier reef paralleling the coast forms a maze of chutes, surge channels, and pourovers, some of it fairly protected and accessible. Other parts require the same precise maneuvering and judgment of kayaking as whitewater rivers do—producing the same level of thrills mixed with the same level of danger. And then, of course, there are the sharks (see "Paddling the Red Triangle"). Rugged and remote, this rock garden play spot is not everyone's cup of sea, but skilled paddlers with an adrenaline habit will find it addicting.

TRIP HIGHLIGHTS: Excellent rock garden play spot, seabirds, solitude, and scenery.

TRIP RATING:

Intermediate: 1–5 miles, recommended only for those with previous open-coast experience and only *in the company of an*

advanced paddler, during low tide when swells are below 3–4 feet and winds below 15 knots.

Advanced: 5 miles of open coast with excellent rock garden play in swells to 6 feet; not recommended above 8 feet when waves wash over protective outer reefs.

TRIP DURATION: Part to full day.

NAVIGATION AIDS: USGS *Pigeon Point and Franklin Point* (7.5 minute). Wx radio: "Pigeon Point to Piedras Blancas"; buoys: Pillar Point and Pigeon Point.

TIDAL INFORMATION: In general the lower the tide, the more protection the reef gives.

CAUTIONS: Fog so thick you can't see shore from beyond the surf zone, strong wind, waves, and submerged rocks. You must pick your day, especially if planning to play in rock gardens: Waves crashing on rocks can be, *and have been,* lethal to kayakers. As close as this area is to the highway, it is surprisingly remote; if you have trouble on the water, you're a long way from help. Before entering rock gardens, consider how you will do a rescue if someone capsizes. A solid combat roll is highly recommended here for two reasons: first, in tighter rock gardens, other forms of capsize recovery may be impossible; second, the area is barely 2 miles from the elephant seal rookery at Año Nuevo where many great white sharks have been identified and tagged, so it's not the best place to be out of your boat. As for elephant seals, while uncommon, we were once confronted at Whitehouse by a 14-foot, one-ton, territorial male, forcing us to land elsewhere.

TRIP PLANNING: For a first visit smaller swell and lower tide offer more protection for exploration behind the reefs. For a thrill the best conditions are a 4- to 6-foot northwest swell and a 3- to 4-foot tide height, allowing waves to wash over and through slots in the reefs. This forms the best runs through *surge channels* and *pourovers* (if not sure what these terms mean, go with someone who does). Scout Whitehouse Creek by foot first to check landing conditions, to help recognize the beach from seaward, and to pick a line through the rocks. Run a shuttle for a north-south trip and save energy for the 0.25-mile carry or launch and land at the south end (on windy days, we often launch from Whitehouse and spend the entire day playing in the rock gardens in the lee of Franklin Point).

LAUNCH SITE: On Highway 1, 1 mile north of Pigeon Point Lighthouse, where the lighthouse road rejoins the highway, is a dirt road pull out to a sandy beach in the lee of Bolsa Point. No fees/facilities. **Alternate launch sites:** Gazos Creek State Beach, 1 mile south of the lighthouse is okay on calm days, but it has little protection and rocks in the surf zone. There is free parking and outhouses. Whitehouse Creek is a small, unsigned dirt pull out at a state park trailhead 1 mile south of Gazos. Look for some roadside mailboxes across from the Skylark Ranch sign. Free parking, no facilities.

DIRECTIONS

START: From the beach at **Bolsa Point,** head south along the bluffs toward the lighthouse. *Caution:* Numerous offshore boomers along this stretch. The safest route is well out beyond them.

MILE 1.0: Just south of **Pigeon Point Lighthouse**, seas should get calmer. *Caution:* Confused seas, submerged rocks, and reefs extend well out to sea off the point. In the lee of the point, stay well right of the sea stacks and the seals hauled out on them.

MILE 3.0: Gazos Creek gives access to a 1-mile-long stretch of sandy beach punctuated by dumping surf and the occasional submerged rock.

MILE 4.0: Sandy beach gives way to the jagged black rock of **Franklin Point.** *Caution:* Stay well outside the point and watch for boomers. As protection increases and conditions grow calmer in the lee, the best rock gardens begin.

MILE 4.5: A narrow, rocky opening leads into a calm cove with protected rock gardens and a sandy beach for a rest break. It also has long trail access to road.

MILE 4.75: Another smaller cove for landing and a trail.

MILE 5.0: Take out at **Whitehouse Creek**; kayak surfing is available off the reefs to the south.

Where to Eat & Where to Stay

RESTAURANTS   Twenty miles south, **Davenport's Gray Whale City Bakery Bar and Grill** (831–423–9803) serves sandwiches in addition to baked goods. Twenty-five miles north, **Tres Amigos** (831–423–9803) taqueria in Half Moon Bay serves fast, hearty Mexican food. (Also see Route 24: Pillar Point & Beyond.)
LODGING   Pigeon Point Lighthouse youth hostel requires reservations on summer weekends; consider making them two months in advance (415–879–0633). (Also see Route 24: Pillar Point & Beyond.)   **CAMPING**   Sites are available among the redwoods at **Butano State Park**; call Park Net (800–444–7275) for information. (Also see Route 24: Pillar Point Harbor & Beyond.)

Bolsa
Point

P

Lighthouse Rd

Lighthouse/
Hostel

1

Pigeon
Point

seal
rocks

N

PIGEON POINT
to Franklin Point

0   1

miles

PACIFIC

OCEAN

P

Gazos Creek

1

dunes

Franklin
Point

TO
SANTA
CRUZ

*Whitehouse
Creek*

P

Franklin Point

FRANKLIN POINT
ROCK GARDENS

*Whitehouse
Creek*

Paddling the Red Triangle: White Shark Fact & Fiction

Nothing puts the *wild* in *wilderness*, we've heard said,
like the presence of some large and fangy alpha
predator. Alaska has its grizzlies, the Serengetti its lions,
and the Central Coast its great white sharks. But what are
the actual risks to kayakers? True the area between the
elephant seal rookeries at Año Nuevo, the Farallon
Islands, and Point Reyes is known as the "Red Triangle,"
an area of ocean that's had more attacks on humans than
any other on earth. However it's not necessarily a shark
breeding ground, as locals often proclaim. Truth is, shark
scientists don't know where whites go to breed. Anyway
it's not *breeding* that presents a problem but *feeding*, so
an understanding of sharks' hunting behavior is probably
your best defense. Elephant seals are the sharks' favorite
prey, so they like to hunt around seal colonies. Sharks
generally attack from below with one lightning-like strike,
then back off and wait for the seal to bleed to death.
This hit-and-run technique protects them from injury, as

shark researchers, who photo ID the animals, have noted teeth marks on some sharks where seals have bitten back with their bear-sized canines. The movie *Jaws* aside, white sharks are not "eating machines" (one seal may last a shark days or even weeks), nor are they "man-eaters." Of the millions of people who take to our waters each year, very few end up on the menu. Typically two or three divers or surfers annually get attacked in the Triangle, and they usually survive to tell the tale when the shark, perhaps expecting tasty blubber instead of neoprene, doesn't return to finish the meal. Poor eyesight is the likely culprit; shark eyes probably distinguish little more than seal-shaped silhouettes, so forget anything you may have heard about their attraction to "yum-yum yellow." So far, knock on wood, no full-length touring kayaks have been hit; perhaps from below they appear as a full-grown bull elephant seal—no easy meal. In recent years only two kayaks have been mistaken in this area: Both were short boats (a 12-foot river kayak and an 8-foot sit-on-top), both were near seal colonies at points in the Triangle (Año Nuevo and Bodega Head), and both paddlers were uninjured. Your chances of getting struck by lightning are probably a hundred times better than becoming shark bait; however you do increase your odds by climbing around on the lightning rod in a thunder storm. To lower your risks, stay away from seal colonies or paddle with partners in shorter boats (we call them "chum boats"), and by far the most dangerous part of your paddling day will be the drive home.

Route 26:

━━ ━━ ━━ ━━ ━━ ━━ ━━ ━━ ━━ ━━ ━━ ━━ ➤

Santa Cruz Harbor to Natural Bridges State Beach & Beyond

Point Santa Cruz, better known locally as Lighthouse Point, forms the northern boundary of Monterey Bay and creates a wide arc of semisheltered water for kayakers. Aspiring intermediates will find good protection from prevailing wind and seas most days, making this area an excellent choice for a first trip onto open water. Sea lions, seals, and otters frequent these waters, along with many of the area's best board surfers, who are drawn to the world-famous waves that curl around the point. Exposure increases rapidly as you paddle northward toward Natural Bridges State Beach. Beyond it lie some of the sanctuary's wilder shores.

TRIP HIGHLIGHTS: Relatively protected ocean paddling, marine mammals, and seabirds.

TRIP RATING:

Beginner: 1 mile inside harbor, watch for boat traffic; on calm days advanced beginners with open-water rescue skills and an intermediate in the lead may find suitable conditions as far as Lighthouse Point, a 3-mile round-trip.

Intermediate: 3–5 miles. Lighthouse Point with a surf landing on Cowell Beach is generally protected enough in swells to 4 feet and winds to 15 knots; if these conditions hold beyond the point, you might continue to Mitchell Cove.

Advanced: 5–16 miles of remote, exposed cliffs to Natural Bridges and beyond to 4 Mile Beach, with rock gardens, surf breaks, and caves.

TRIP DURATION: Part to full day.

NAVIGATION AIDS: USGS *Santa Cruz* (7.5 minute) and NOAA chart 18685. Wx radio: "Monterey Bay boaters' forecast"; buoys: Santa Cruz, Monterey, and Pigeon Point.

TIDAL INFORMATION: Little effect; some low-tide beaches beyond Natural Bridges.

CAUTIONS: Tricky harbor entrance: Narrow mouth with "blind spot" behind jetty makes approaching boat traffic difficult to see; waves break in mouth during certain conditions. There are occasional offshore winds, fog, and sneaker waves. Landing is prohibited except on the west end of Cowell Beach, Mitchell Cove, and the north end of Natural Bridges.

TRIP PLANNING: Scout harbor mouth from shore before launching to assess sea conditions. Less wind generally makes mornings safer, assuming it's not too foggy to see.

LAUNCH SITE: To reach harbor boat ramp from Highway 1, take Soquel Street exit west to 7th Street and turn away from the freeway and hills, following signs to Santa Cruz Small Craft Harbor. Turn right on Eaton Street, left on Lake Avenue just before crossing the harbor bridge, and follow signs to the launch ramp at the far right end of the parking lot. Launch from ramp or off dock. Parking, $5.00/vehicle; public rest rooms available. Alternate launch sites: Cowell Beach okay midweek, but parking is tough on weekends; Mitchell Cove or Natural Bridges for surf savvy paddlers.

DIRECTIONS

START: Cross to the far right side of the boat channel and follow the jetty to the harbor mouth. Once outside the harbor, head right along the beach, but keep your distance: Boats are prohibited within 500 feet of shore. *Caution:* Watch for boat traffic and waves at harbor mouth. *Sidetrip:* Head left from the harbor and round Pleasure Point to Capitola (see rte. 27).

MILE 1.0: Skirt the end of the **Municipal Wharf**, looking for sea lions on the pilings, but keep your distance from them and fishing lines. *Caution:* Boats prohibited within 50 yards of wharf (except at the kayak rental dock—Venture Quest; 831–427–2267—toward the shoreward end).

Santa Cruz Harbor   *-143-*

Sidetrip: Assuming the surf is small, and you have a helmet and some surf zone training, landing is allowed on the far left of Cowell Beach.

MILE 1.5: Look for otters and sea lions along the kelp beds or watch the surfers at world-renowned **Steamer Lane**. *Caution:* Keep your distance from the cliffs: Territorial board surfers have been know to hurl insults, and sneaker waves have washed several kayaks into the cliffs. *Sidetrip:* Paddle out to the sea lion rocks off **Lighthouse Point**.

MILE 2.75: There is a fairly protected landing at **Mitchell Cove**. *Sidetrip:* Advanced paddlers with bomber rolls might try the rock gardens east of the cove, but be careful: One of the authors received a memorable trashing there once.

MILE 4.0: **Natural Bridges**, the last beach in town, makes a good landing spot for those with strong surf zone skills, and a good alternate launch site for advanced trips up the rugged north coast.

OTHER OPTIONS: Experienced open-coast paddlers can paddle north along the cliffs from Natural Bridges on calm days. (From Highway 1, north of town, take Swift Street and follow signs.) Landings are few and remote, and strong winds with rough seas are common. Sandy and inviting, **Wilder Beach,** 2 miles north, is closed to protect nesting habitat for endangered snowy plovers. Smaller pocket beaches in the next mile are possible but challenging. The best protection can be found at **3 Mile Beach** and **4 Mile Beach**, respectively, at the suggested mileage. The extremely exposed 10-mile, one-way trip from Davenport Landing to Natural Bridges makes an excellent expedition for experts. Speaking of exposure, en route camping is possible at Red White and Blue Beach, a private "Clothing Optional" campground around mile 5.

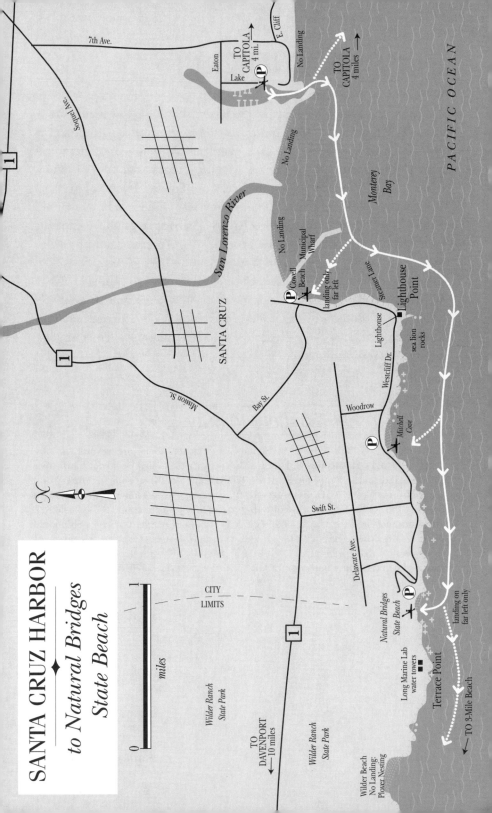

Sooty Shearwaters

We're half mile offshore about to practice open-water rescues with our surf zone class when we first see the birds. Skimming low across the water, first hundreds—*then thousands upon thousands*—of dark gray birds looking like chubby sea gulls engulf us like a swarm of giant bees. Within moments the flock is so thick it blocks our view of others in our group. "Sooty shearwaters," calls out Steve, a friend of ours who teaches birding classes, "among the most numerous birds on Earth." Shearwaters are a pelagic (open-ocean) species, Steve explains later, that spends most of its life at sea, except for a few months of our winter when they breed on land in the Southern Hemisphere. After that the birds head to sea, chasing summer and schools of fish across the North Pacific in flocks numbering into the tens or even hundreds of thousands. Deep water near shore rich in prey draws them into Monterey Bay, where they can sometimes be seen from the beach. Or from the seat of a kayak.

Where to Eat & Where to Stay

RESTAURANTS In Santa Cruz Harbor, there are several options, including **Rosa's Rosticeria** (831–479–3536) with cafeteria-style Mexican food, roast chicken, and seafood specialties. A few blocks away on the corner of Murray and Seabright are **Costa Brava** (831–423–8190), an inexpensive taqueria; the **Seabright Brewery** (831–426–2739), for great pub grazing; and **Java Junction** (831–423–5282), with smoothies and treats. **LODGING** Santa Cruz harbor has a **Shipboard Boat & Breakfast** (831–457–1645) and countless hotels. Call the **chamber of commerce** at (831) 423–1111. **CAMPING** RV travelers can use the **RV parking lot in the upper harbor** by calling the office at (831) 475–6161. (See also Route 27: Pleasure Point.)

Route 27:

━ ━ ━ ━ ━ ━ ━ ━ ━ ━ ━ ━ ━ ━ ➤

In the Lee of Pleasure Point: Capitola, New Brighton, & Seacliff Beaches

The most protected stretch of "open coast" on Monterey Bay, the lee of Soquel Point, better known locally as Pleasure Point, makes an excellent first coastal tour for those comfortable launching and landing through small surf. In the kelp beds beyond the cliffs, sea otters and harbor seals are commonly seen, and occasionally bottlenose dolphin. For more experienced paddlers, the longboat surfing off several reef breaks is some of the best anywhere.

TRIP HIGHLIGHTS: Semiprotected coastal paddling, wildlife, scenery, and surfing.

TRIP RATING:

Beginner: 1–2 miles on calm days with no small surf at the launch beach.

Intermediate: 5+ miles round-trip to Pleasure Point requires open-water paddling skills and basic surf zone skills to negotiate the beaches. Not recommended if surf at New Brighton above 2–3 feet when dumping shorebreak can be difficult to dangerous.

Advanced: 10 miles round-trip to Santa Cruz harbor. Surfing at reef breaks along cliffs for those with bomber rolls, with clean shoulders in waves from 3 to 8 feet or more.

TRIP DURATION: Part to full day.

NAVIGATION AIDS: USGS *Soquel* (7.5 minute). Wx radio: "Monterey Bay boaters' forecast"; buoys: Santa Cruz and Monterey.

TIDAL INFORMATION: Tide heights less than 3 or 4 feet offer greater access to small beaches along cliffs.

CAUTIONS: Submerged rocks (boomers) and waves on reefs,

especially on falling tide; board surfers, swimmers; no landing on Capitola Beach (east side of wharf); local afternoon winds sometimes blow from the east (up to 15 knots) against the usual northwest trend, causing choppy seas and making return to launch site a slog. A dropping tide can create surf at the landing beach that wasn't there when you launched. Be extremely careful of surf and rocks if attempting to land on beaches at the base of cliffs.

TRIP PLANNING: Paddle early to beat wind, and, on busy summer weekends, to beat the beach crowds and find better parking. A low but rising tide will make boomers more numerous but easier to locate. Stay beyond the kelp to avoid sneaker waves on the reefs.

LAUNCH SITE: New Brighton State Beach has a large parking lot on bluffs above beach and is well worth the $6.00 entry fee despite the long carry down the stairs to beach. From Highway 1 on the south side of Santa Cruz, take the Park Avenue/New Brighton exit and follow signs toward beach. Take a left at first stop sign at Kennedy Street, then the first right into the park. Alternate launch sites: Capitola Wharf, but its parking is limited, especially on weekends. Seacliff Beach offers less protection and bigger surf, and lifeguards sometimes deny launching access on busy weekends when swimmers crowd the surf.

DIRECTIONS

START: Launch from far right (west) side of **New Brighton Beach**, where the surf tends to be smaller, but stay well away from rocks at the base of cliffs. Head west along sandstone cliffs, with the safest route being well out along the kelp beds where otters are common. Several low-tide beaches dot the cliffs from here to Pleasure Point. *Caution:* Stay well offshore, many shallow reefs cause intermittent waves to break up to several hundred yards from shore, making this a popular board surfing area and a tricky place to land a kayak. Access to beaches can be deceptively difficult in all but the smallest swells. *Sidetrip:* Advanced paddlers with strong surfing skills and reliable Eskimo roll may find good surfing conditions on reef breaks away from board surfers.

MILE 1.0: You can land on the small beach on the far (west) side of **Capitola Wharf,** or use the seasonal dingy dock on the pier from May

In the Lee of Pleasure Point

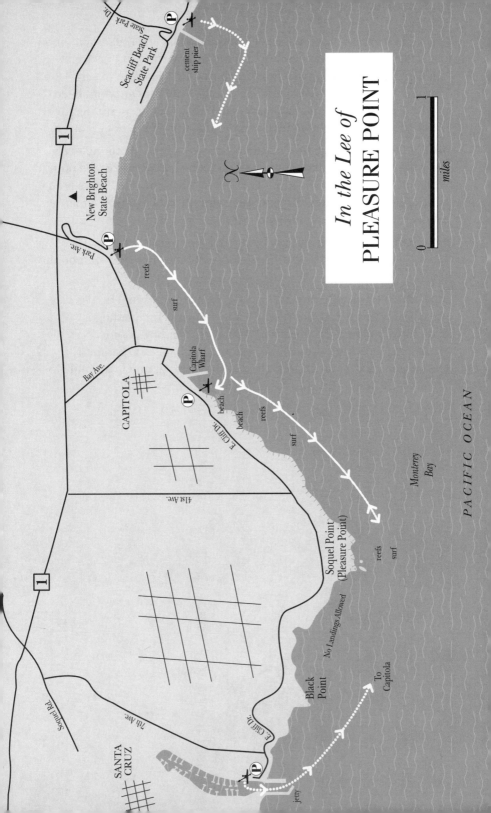

In the Lee of PLEASURE POINT

miles

0   1

PACIFIC OCEAN

Monterey Bay

Seacliff Beach State Park

State Park Dr.

cement ship pier

1

New Brighton State Beach

Park Ave.

reefs

surf

CAPITOLA

Bay Ave.

Capitola Wharf

E. Cliff Dr.

beach

beach

reefs

surf

41st Ave.

Soquel Point (Pleasure Point)

reefs

surf

No Landings Allowed

Black Point

To Capitola

E. Cliff Dr.

1

SANTA CRUZ

Soquel Rd.

7th Ave.

jetty

through October. On summer weekends the Wharf House restaurant on the wharf serves alfresco lunches with live jazz on their sun deck. *Caution:* Landing on the west side beach can be dangerous in surf because waves tend to sweep into the pilings. Landings are prohibited on the main part of **Capitola Beach** east of the pier except during the off-season, when, if no swimmers are present, this rule is not enforced.

MILE 1.25: The first small, cliff-side beach west of the pier is generally deserted and easy to land on in small surf. The reef break off the point is a good entry-level surfing spot in waves to 3 feet provided there are no board surfers in the area. Beyond this point the reef extends out farther, so watch out for sneaker waves and surfers.

MILE 2.0: This first obvious minor point is a popular surf spot, **The Hook,** at the end of 41st Avenue. Pleasure Point is the next point on the horizon.

MILE 2.5: **Pleasure Point** makes a good turn-around spot because seas are typically much rougher on the windward side, and landing is prohibited between the point and Santa Cruz Harbor. *Sidetrip:* Experienced paddlers can continue another 2.5 miles to Santa Cruz Harbor for a lunch break and return with the wind, or run a shuttle for a one-way downwind trip to Capitola (see rte. 26).

Cement Ship

Built during WWI when steel was in short supply, the S.S. *Palo Alto*, better known as "The Cement Ship," at Seacliff Beach never saw action. By the time the ship was finished, so was the war. Investors brought the ship to Seacliff in 1930, flooded the bilges so it would rest solidly on the shallow bottom, extended a pier out to meet the ship, and turned it into an amusement center, complete with arcade, swimming pool, dining hall, and ballroom. Operating successfully as "The Ship" for two summers, she faced two devastating winters. The 1932 storms cracked her hull, closing The Ship. Four years later the *Palo Alto* was sold to the state for one dollar, eventually to become part of the Seacliff Beach State Park. The pier remains a popular fishing spot, while the Cement Ship slowly deteriorates with the waves, its seaward portion fenced off to provide for the safety of the curious public, and a haven for harbor seals and seabirds, especially the once threatened brown pelicans.

Where to Eat & Where to Stay

RESTAURANTS   **Margaritaville** (831–476–2263), a trendy Mexican restaurant and bar, is one of many choices along the Capitola Beach waterfront. **LODGING**   **Capitola Beach Rentals** (831–476–1991) rents cottages and beach houses. There are many hotels nearby; the closest are **Best Western Seacliff Inn** (831–688–7300) or **Capitola Venetian Inn** (831–476–6471).   **CAMPING**   New **Brighton State Beach** has attractive tent camping on the bluffs among the Monterey pines for $14 to $23 per night or "en route camping." Hiker/biker sites are available at $3.00 per person for those kayaking in, but the carry from the beach to the campground is a long one, uphill for half a mile. **Seacliff Beach State Park** offers tightly packed, beachfront camping for RVs. Both parks fill quickly within the seven-month maximum reservation period. Call Park Net (800–444–7275) for information and reservations.

Route 28:

----------------------------------->

Elkhorn Slough National Estuarine Research Reserve: Moss Landing to Rubis Creek

Winding some 7 miles from the sea into rolling coastal hills, Elkhorn Slough is California's second-largest marine wetland after San Francisco Bay and one of only twenty National Estuarine Reserves in the country. In addition to being one of the best places to view seals and sea otters from a kayak—sightings are essentially guaranteed— the slough is a major feeding ground for migratory birds on the West Coast. Its fertile mudflats and salt marshes support an incredible diversity of marine life. Until recently, in fact, Elkhorn Slough held the North American record for the most species of birds sighted in one place on one day, 116. In all, over 300 species reside in the area or migrate throughout the year. The Moss Landing launch site, adjacent to the slough's opening to the sea, is more dynamic than the inland launch site (see Route 29: Kirby Park) having increased tidal flow and more boat traffic.

TRIP HIGHLIGHTS: World-class birding and excellent marine mammal viewing.

TRIP RATING:

Beginner: 1–5 miles during tidal exchanges of less than 3 to 4 feet; experience reading tides recommended.

Intermediate: 5–7+ miles with moderate tide rips during large tide changes; surfing and coastal touring access on days with little wind and swells below 4 feet, but an advanced trip leader is recommended as the ocean can become rough quickly here.

Advanced: 7+ miles of excellent access to surfing and open-coast sidetrips.

TRIP DURATION: Part to full day.

NAVIGATION AIDS: Together with a local tide table, the *Elkhorn Slough Paddling Guide* is invaluable; this free map and informational flyer showing channels, mudflats, and closed areas is available at kayak shops near the launch site (Kayak Connection at 831-724-5692 and Monterey Bay Kayaks at 831-373-5357) or from the Elkhorn Slough Foundation at (831) 728-5939; USGS *Moss Landing* (7.5 minute) for coastal sidetrips. Wx radio: "Monterey Bay boaters' forecast"; buoys: Monterey.

TIDAL INFORMATION: Mudflats make paddling outside the main channel difficult to impossible when tide heights drop below 2 feet; strong currents develop during tide changes over 3 or 4 feet.

CAUTIONS: Tidal currents especially hazardous at the mouth of the slough during strong ebbs. Paddle and land only in designated areas so as not to disturb sensitive habitat; stay far enough from marine mammals and birds not to change their behavior (minimum of 50 feet). Watch for boat traffic and fishing lines in the harbor area and the ubiquitous afternoon winds.

TRIP PLANNING: Use the currents. Days with a morning flood and afternoon ebb are best for heading into the slough from the mouth, but save some energy to fight the afternoon wind on your return. *Note:* Keeping close to the banks lessens the effects of contrary winds or currents. If exploring side channels, do so on a rising tide; beware of countless dead ends; try to follow the widest, deepest branch; and turn around before the branch gets narrower than the length of your boat, or you could have a lot of backing up to do. Also, avoid hitting the banks, which will cover your boat in sticky mud and cause erosion to sensitive habitat.

LAUNCH SITES: From Highway 1, about 0.5 mile north of the bridge over the slough, turn toward the ocean at the sign for Moss Landing Boat Ramp. Use the ramp for a $5.00 fee, or launch for free from the adjacent beach, which can be quite muddy at low tide. Facilities: rest rooms and water. **Alternate launch sites:** Moss Landing State Beach across the water from the boat ramp costs

$3.00, but it only has outhouses and no water. Park at the far end of the dirt parking lot at the end of the road and launch from the beach by the big black oil pipe (once used to fuel the power plant, which now runs on natural gas).

DIRECTIONS

START: Head under **Highway 1 Bridge** and paddle east (left) into slough. *Caution:* Avoid the boat channel (marked by red and green buoys) and fishing lines and watch out for strong currents under the bridge that can sweep you into pilings or even out to sea (if it's ebbing reconsider your tides). *Sidetrips:* Advanced paddlers will generally find challenging (sometimes hazardous) conditions out on Monterey Bay (see Other Options).

MILE 0.5: The **sandy beach** on right is the only landing/lunch spot for 2 miles, but it's private property above high tide.

MILE 1.5: **Seal haul out** on the left bank (north) at the beginning of the big U bend is the only birthing area in the slough and sensitive to disturbance, especially in spring, so keep your distance. Look for otters, sometimes two dozen or more, in the small bay on the left beyond the seal haul out. *Sidetrip:* You can follow a channel into the pickleweed marsh in the back of the otter bay at high tide. The channel mouth can be difficult to spot from a distance. This makes a good turn-around spot for a short trip.

MILE 2.0: After rounding the big bend, the slough straightens out and passes **Moonglow Dairy** on the right (south) side just opposite the narrower of two openings to Rubis Creek. This twisting channel is easier to follow from its other, larger opening (described later), which is 0.5 mile farther on the left (north), where the oak-covered ridge comes closest to the slough.

MILE 2.5: A short way up the larger, eastern entrance to **Rubis Creek** used to give access to a popular lunch stop. Unfortunately this private property is now closed to kayakers until further notice (see www.eskape kayak.com for updates). *Caution:* Slough managers are trying to keep kayakers and kayaks off the fragile mudflat. *Sidetrip:* Return to Moss Landing via the "scenic route" through the twisting channels of Rubis Creek.

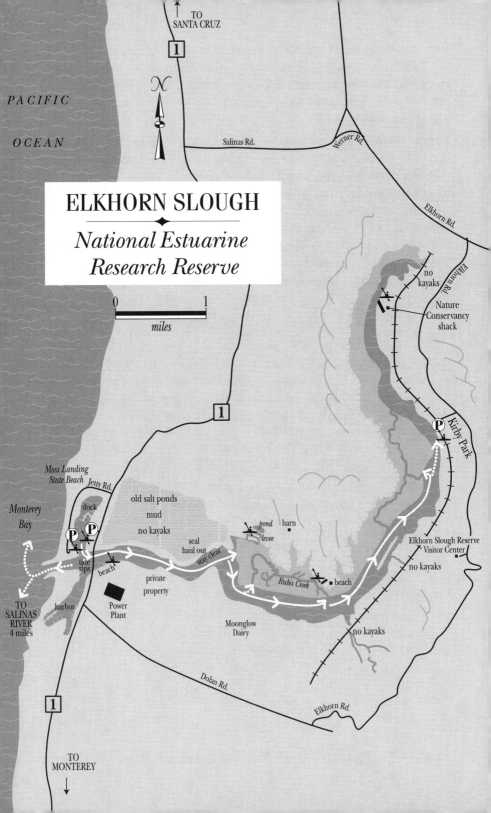

Continue down Rubis Creek's main channel until you get to the "deceptive left," a 90° bend leading to a dead end. Take the smaller right channel straight ahead through a series of narrow S turns (where you'll be sure you are lost) until the channel widens again, bends to the left, and rejoins the slough across from the dairy.

OTHER OPTIONS: Run a shuttle for a one-way trip to Kirby Park on a flood tide with the wind and current behind you most of the way. Advanced paddlers with strong surf zone skills have two main options. The first is to head north up the coast along the broad expanse of dunes for good views of Monterey Bay and surfing. The second is to run a shuttle and paddle 5 miles south to the mouth of the Salinas River, portage across the sandbar to the lagoon (it's 0.25 to 0.5 mile north of the barge wreck), then paddle 2 miles upriver to the Highway 1 bridge (see Route 30: Salinas River). *Caution:* Scout first. The mouth of Moss Landing Harbor can get quite rough, especially during an ebb when strong currents sweep seaward and waves can break inside the mouth along south jetty. Submerged pilings extend off the north jetty. Before heading to the Salinas River, try a touch-and-go landing on the beach off the north jetty; unless this is easy, don't expect to be able to handle the bigger surf at the mouth of the Salinas.

Where to Eat & Where to Stay

RESTAURANTS   You'll find good California-style Mexican food at **Whole Enchilada** (831–633–3038), on the west side of Highway 1 just south of the bridge. If you turn off the highway toward the ocean past the Whole Enchilada, you will be on the road to **Phil's Smoke Shack & Deli** (831–633–1775) to buy fresh fish to go or stay and eat a good meal. **Maloney's Harbor Inn** (831–724–9371) has good seafood and is located next to the Highway 1 bridge near the launch ramp. **LODGING**   There are no lodgings nearby. (See Route 26: Santa Cruz Harbor and Route 31: Monterey.) **CAMPING**   Camping at the slough is "en route camping" in the parking lot for self-contained vehicles only, but **Sunset Beach State Park**, 5 miles north, has tent and RV sites on bluffs above the bay. Call Park Net for reservations (800–444–7275).

Marine Mammals:
Sea Lion, Seal, or Otter?

One of the skills expected of kayakers in this area, it seems, is the ability to distinguish between sea lions, seals, and otters. California sea lions *(Zalophus californianus)* are what most people picture as the typical "circus seal," sitting upright with a ball balanced on its slender snout. Their familiar doglike bark sets them apart from their generally silent cousins. Sea lions become much larger, with fully grown adult bulls in the eight-foot, 800-pound range, and tend to be brownish-blond in color. A particularly distinguishing characteristic is that their rear flippers rotate forward, allowing them to sit upright and "walk." Kayakers typically see them barking on rocks, swimming fast and "porpoising" up and out of the water, or floating on the surface with one flipper in the air thermoregulating and looking unnervingly like a shark's fin. Harbor seals *(Phoca vitulina)* are chubbier, looking like four- to six-foot cigars in a variety of colors from black to light gray to speckled. They can't turn their rear flippers to walk, so they squirm along on their bellies. Typically seen basking prone on rocks or beaches, the shy but curious creatures also like to float with just their head showing as they sneak up behind your kayak. Sea otters *(Enhydra lutris)* rarely take to land and can be distinguished from harbor seals because they tend to float on their backs, often smacking shellfish open against a rock on their chest, with a telltale gull floating nearby to steal scraps.

Route 29:

━━ ━━ ━━ ━━ ━━ ━━ ━━ ━━ ━━ ━━ ━━ ➤

Upper Elkhorn Slough— Kirby Park Area

More sheltered than the slough's ocean end (see rte. 28 for a full description of Elkhorn Slough), the inland waters around Kirby Park make a better trip for mellow beginners or on days when there are strong tidal currents elsewhere in the slough. Although you're less likely to see seals and otters this far up the slough, the birding is still excellent. Extensive mudflats and pickleweed marshes make prime shorebird habitat, and the surrounding oak forests and grasslands are the preferred haunts of raptors, owls, and numerous other woodland species. More ambitious paddlers can take the "slough to sea" route, riding the tides all the way to Moss Landing.

TRIP HIGHLIGHTS: World-class birding and protected waterways.

TRIP RATING:

Beginner: 1–5+ miles during tidal exchanges less than 3 or 4 feet; experience reading tides recommended.

Intermediate: 1–10-mile round-trip to Moss Landing with moderate tide rips during big tide changes.

TRIP DURATION: Part to full day.

NAVIGATION AIDS: Together with a local tide table, the *Elkhorn Slough Paddling Guide* is invaluable; this free map and informational flyer showing channels, mudflats, and closed areas is available at kayak shops in Moss Landing or from the Elkhorn Slough Foundation at (831) 728–5939. Wx radio: "Monterey Bay boaters' forecast"; buoys: Monterey.

TIDAL INFORMATION: Mudflats make paddling outside the main channel difficult to impossible when tide heights drop below 2 feet; strong currents develop during tide changes over 3 or 4 feet.

CAUTIONS: Check the tides: Falling water can strand you in the mud, and strong currents can cause problems, especially at the mouth of the slough. Paddle and land only in designated areas so as not to disturb the sensitive habitat, and stay far enough from marine mammals and birds (minimum of 50 feet) not to change their behavior. Expect strong afternoon winds.

TRIP PLANNING: Paddle early morning or late afternoon to avoid wind. High, rising tides leave more room to explore with less chance of getting stuck in mud, especially if exploring side channels. In channels, beware of countless dead ends; try to follow the widest, deepest branch; and turn around before it gets narrower than the length of your boat, or you could have a lot of backing up to do. Also, avoid hitting the banks, which will cover your boat in sticky mud and cause erosion to sensitive habitat.

LAUNCH SITE: From Highway 1 just south of the Moss Landing Bridge, take Dolan Road east to Elkhorn Road, turn left and follow it 5 miles to Kirby Park. If you are coming south from Santa Cruz on Highway 1, take Salinas Road east (about 5 miles north of Moss Landing), turn right on Werner Road, right again onto Elkhorn Road, and follow the signs to Kirby Park. Free parking, outhouses, but no water.

DIRECTIONS

START: Paddle to the right and take your time investigating the pickleweed marsh on the left bank. *Sidetrip:* Venture to the left for a longer trip to **Rubis Creek** or **Moss Landing** (see rte. 28).

MILE 1.0: Nature Conservancy shack on the right with a wooden dock made for kayakers to climb out on. A little hard to find at first, the third channel from the right leads to the dock (**GPS N 36° 51' 03", W 121° 45' 30"**). There is no outhouse here but lots of tall grass and privacy. *Caution:* Tide height above 2 feet is necessary for access.

MILE 2.5: Access to the upper slough ends at the railroad trestle. Time to turn around and wander back.

OTHER OPTIONS: Leaving a shuttle vehicle at Moss Landing makes a great one-way trip, which we call "slough to sea." With a nice morning ebb, kayaks will drift the 5 miles before lunch. More ambitious paddlers can catch the flood tide back to Kirby after lunch for a 10-mile round-trip. *Caution:* Beware of strong currents funneling under the Highway 1 bridge.

Where to Eat & Where to Stay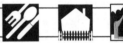

RESTAURANTS, LODGING, & CAMPING

See Route 28: Elkhorn Slough: Moss Landing for recommendations.

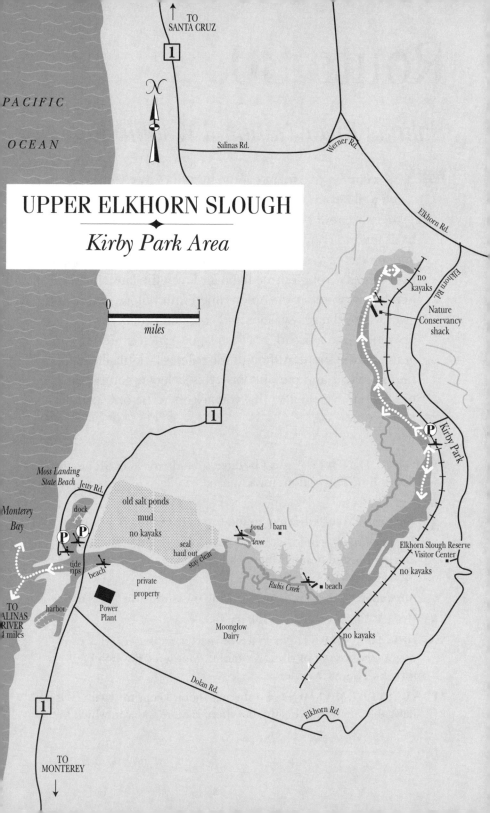

Route 30:

— — — — — — — — — — — — ➤

Salinas River National Wildlife Refuge

The secluded marshland at the mouth of the Salinas River is a well-known hot spot among local birders. Although there are fewer species here than at Elkhorn Slough, the birds tend to concentrate in large flocks by the river mouth and are easier to spot. Peaceful and remote, this short span of river passes through three habitats: From the launch area, a nearly freshwater environment lined with willows and reeds gives way to flat grassy fields and coastal scrub, before opening up to a broad, brackish lagoon surrounded by dunes at the Pacific shore. Although the Salinas lacks facilities (boat ramps, toilets, and parking lots), this lack of amenities is made up for by the fact that you are often the only paddlers on the water.

TRIP HIGHLIGHTS: great birding, solitude, views of Monterey Bay, and surfing options for advanced paddlers.

TRIP RATING:

Beginner: Protected 4-mile round-trip to river mouth.

Intermediate: 4+ miles with good surf zone practice and coastal touring possibilities on Monterey Bay in waves below 3 feet and winds to 15 knots.

Advanced: 4+ miles with good surfing off sandbar in waves to 6 feet.

TRIP DURATION: Part to full day.

NAVIGATION AIDS: No charts or maps necessary on this easily negotiated stretch of river. Wx radio: "Monterey Bay boaters' forecast"; buoys: Monterey.

TIDAL INFORMATION: Freshwater inflow keeps the main channel navigable at any tide height, but there is more water in which to

explore shallow areas during higher tides. Currents are generally
weak except during the occasional flood year when the river
breaches the sandbar separating it from the ocean (see Cautions).

CAUTIONS: Expect strong afternoon winds. Overgrown banks make
landing difficult except at the mouth, and landing is prohibited
entirely on the left bank (south) because of the bird refuge. The
irony is that duck hunting is permitted from mid-October to mid-
January, so be aware of blinds and hunters. (This is not a popular
hunting area, and you will be in their way, not vice versa. *Note:*
Serious birders won't add decoys to their life list.) After big rains
banks get slick and muddy at the launch site; obviously avoid the
river in flood. In years when the river is open to the sea, expect a
slight current, especially during ebb tide, and stay out of the
channel at the mouth to avoid getting swept into the surf. If the
current is strong at the put in, only those with experience in
currents should consider paddling.

TRIP PLANNING: Head down river early to avoid afternoon winds
(which will be at your back on the return). Depending on water
level, it's interesting to explore the narrow channels between
islands, but sandbars and shallows can slow progress, and the
deepest water is generally found from midchannel to the left
(south) bank. Tidal ranges will be greater if the river is open to the
sea. Calm conditions and scads of migratory birds make fall the
best time of year for paddling and birding; summer is also good,
but there are fewer species. Winter and spring are great for
birding, but higher water levels can be dicey.

Salinas River National Wildlife Refuge

LAUNCH SITE: On Highway 1, 1 mile south of the 156 junction in Castroville, take the Nashua Road exit, crossing over Highway 1 (east). Take the first right onto Monte Road (south) just before the railroad tracks, then follow it for 0.5 mile to the north side of the Salinas River Bridge. On the left before you cross the bridge is a small trailer court. Take the dirt road that skirts along the right-hand edge of the trailer court and follow it down to the small pull out by the river bank beneath the railroad bridge. No fee, no facilities.

START: Head west under the **Salinas River Bridge** and down river. *Sidetrip:* Head 1 mile or so upriver and look for birds in the willows and reeds. Although you can paddle a hundred miles up river, the scenery gets no better as you continue into flat cropland.

MILE 1.0: Look for birdlife hidden in the bushes and reeds along both banks and on midriver islets, but please refrain from landing or walking on these fragile islets.

MILE 2.0: At the river mouth look for a spot along the right (north) bank to land. Choose one where you won't flush the flocks of birds that tend to congregate there. *Caution:* Stay well to the right and out of the channel in the mouth if it is open to the sea unless you have strong surf zone skills. Avoid walking in the signed area in the dunes where endangered snowy plovers nest. Hike over the berm 50 yards or so for great views of the Monterey Bay and the ocean birds—cormorants, surf scoters, and sandpipers—plying the waves, shore, and air or resting on the wreck of the barge 0.25 mile to the south. Dolphins and seals are sometimes seen here as well. *Sidetrip:* Those with helmets and surf zone skills can go for a coastal paddle north along the dunes or try surfing the sandbar at the river mouth, which can be fun in calm conditions but full of rip currents when the surf is up.

Where to Eat & Where to Stay

RESTAURANTS, LODGING, & CAMPING
There are no facilities nearby. (See Route 28: Elkhorn Slough or Route 31: Monterey.)

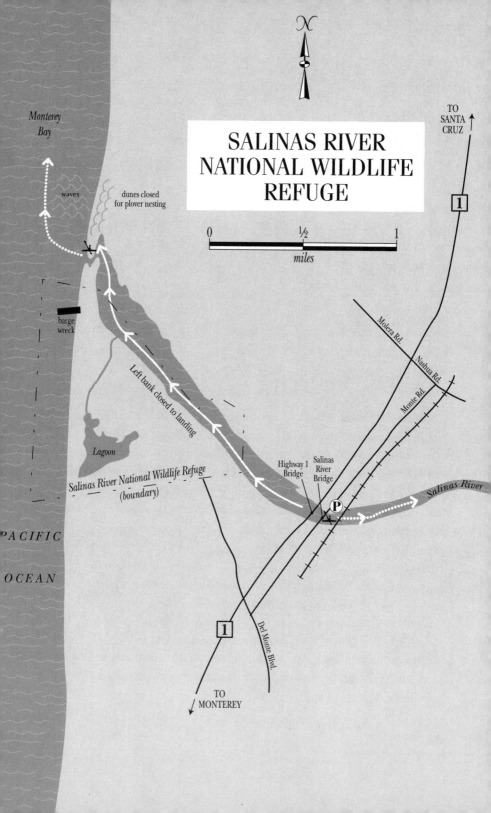

N

Monterey
Bay

waves

dunes closed
for plover nesting

SALINAS RIVER
NATIONAL WILDLIFE
REFUGE

TO
SANTA
CRUZ

1

0   ½   1

miles

barge
wreck

Molera Rd.

Nashua Rd.

Monte Rd.

Left bank closed to landing

Lagoon

Salinas River National Wildlife Refuge
(boundary)

Highway 1
Bridge

Salinas
River
Bridge

P

Salinas River

PACIFIC

OCEAN

1

Del Monte Blvd.

TO
MONTEREY

White Pelicans

Unlike their cousin the California brown pelican, American white pelicans are a rare sight along the seashore. Brilliant snow-white plumage with distinctive black wing tips helps distinguish these birds from their dingier brown namesakes, as does their size—with a wingspan of up to 9½ feet, white pelicans are some 20 percent larger. Perhaps the most interesting of the differences is the white's cooperative feeding behavior. Instead of diving singly for fish, white pelicans "herd" them. Groups of a dozen or so birds circle a school of fish, flailing their wings as the circle closes and driving the fish into a concentrated mass, which greatly increases feeding success as the birds swim into the center, scooping fish into their gular pouches. From August through January look for white pelicans at the mouth of the Salinas River, Elkhorn Slough, Morro Bay, Walker Creek in Tomales Bay, and Drakes Estero.

Route 31:

Monterey's Cannery Row
to Point Piños & Beyond

Nestled in the lee of Point Piños, Monterey's waterfront is one of the few coastal areas protected enough to give beginners access to an ocean paddling environment. Here lush forests of giant kelp harbor a world-renowned diversity of sealife, with near-guaranteed sightings of seals, sea lions, and sea otters. And each winter it's not uncommon for paddlers to spot migrating gray whales. In addition to wildlife viewing, this area is excellent for skills development. Sea conditions change gradually from the lakelike calm inside Monterey Harbor to the full exposure of the open Pacific as you paddle toward Point Piños or beyond. These changes allow paddlers to progress by degrees, enticing them to return repeatedly to improve their skills, stamina, and comfort level.

TRIP HIGHLIGHTS: Excellent marine mammal viewing, ocean birding, whale watching in season, and skill building.

TRIP RATING:

Beginner: 2–5 miles, depending on conditions. Generally a good turn-around spot is the end of Cannery Row before Point Cabrillo about 2 miles each way. On calm days beginners may go all the way to Lovers Cove, especially if accompanied by an intermediate paddler. Even on rough days there is usually enough shelter that if you can get through the small surf at the launch beach, you can paddle for nearly 2 miles—out to the harbor mouth and inside the protection of the harbor breakwater. Helmets and a beginning surf zone class are recommended on days when surf is more than 1 foot.

Intermediate: A 5-mile round trip to Lovers Point is accessible most days, and a 7-mile round-trip to Point Piños is possible when seas are less than 6 feet and winds below 15 knots. For surf zone practice paddle east from the launch area down Del Monte Beach. Waves will grow gradually larger the farther you go.

Advanced: 7–17 miles. Head to Point Piños and back, exploring near-shore rock gardens along the way. Experienced open-coast paddlers with strong water-reading skills, rough-water rescue skills, and good sea sense can run a shuttle to Carmel and round Monterey Peninsula for a seaside view of the famous 17-Mile Drive.

TRIP DURATION: Part to full day.

NAVIGATION AIDS: USGS *Monterey* (7.5 minute) and NOAA chart 18685. Wx radio: "Monterey Bay boaters' forecast"; buoys: Monterey and Point Piños .

TIDAL INFORMATION: During extreme highs some small landing beaches may be covered.

CAUTIONS: Occasional small surf at launch beach, boat traffic around harbor, offshore winds, and submerged rocks near shore; habituated seals in the harbor have occasionally been reported trying to climb onto kayaks.

TRIP PLANNING: Winds generally calmer in mornings and evenings. Summer weekends can get crowded, especially from 10:00 A.M. to 4:00 P.M. Extreme low tides make for interesting kayak tide pooling along the harbor wall.

LAUNCH SITE: From Highway 1 just north of Monterey, take the Pacific Grove/Del Monte Avenue exit, follow Del Monte south through the stoplight at Camino del Estero, then turn right into the parking lot at Monterey Bay Kayaks (MBK); 831–373–5357. MBK generously encourages kayakers to use their facilities, including launch beach, hot outdoor shower, and gear-rinsing tubs. Their parking is free except on busy days when they need their entire lot for kayak renters and tour guests (please ask first), and you'll have to pay $5.00 in the public lot next door. **Alternate launch sites:** possible on calm days for experienced paddlers from small, rocky beaches near Point Piños on Ocean View Drive (at Coral Street, Otters Cove, and others), but usefulness is highly dependent on conditions. Alternative launch site for beginners: San Carlos Beach.

START: Paddle along the fishing pier from **Del Monte Beach**. *Caution:* Stay well away from pier, watching for fishing lines and for sea lions hauled out on pilings. Paddling below sea lions is dangerous as startled animals, some weighing 600 to 800 pounds, could fall on your lap.

MILE 0.3: **Harbor mouth**. *Caution:* Cross boat lanes carefully and quickly, staying out of the way of other vessels. *Sidetrip:* The loop through the harbor is interesting in its own right and an excellent option on rough days. There's good landing at **Heritage Beach** with access to snacks and public rest rooms on **Fisherman's Wharf**. This is a great place to see harbor seals, but some have become so accustomed to kayakers that their curiosity can become a nuisance if they try to climb aboard. Discourage this by paddling quickly away.

MILE 0.75: Beginning of **Cannery Row** and the kelp forests of the new underwater park. Look for sea otters and marine birds, and watch out for divers in the water. The small beach at the end of the jetty is **San Carlos Beach**, a good landing possibility before Lovers Cove. It has public rest rooms.

MILE 1.5: **Monterey Bay Aquarium** at the end of Cannery Row is a good turn-around place to avoid the rougher seas beyond **Point Cabrillo**. No landings are allowed because all beaches in this area are property of **Hopkin's Marine Lab**. If rounding the point, the sandy beach at the far end of the next inlet (bearing 270°) is Lovers Cove.

MILE 2.5: **Lovers Point** is a good turn-around place because seas continue to build beyond the point. The beach at **Lovers Cove**, with public rest room and snack bar, makes a good lunch stop on calm days. *Cautions:* Stay right if landing to avoid submerged rocks on the left; watch out for swimmers.

MILE 3.5: **Point Piños** is the southern edge of Monterey Bay and has the full feeling of the open coast complete with large swell and submerged rocks that cause "boomers." On calm days exploring rock gardens and landing on pocket beaches along the point may be possible for helmeted paddlers with strong skills. *Sidetrip:* For savvy open-coast paddlers, the 9-mile trip around the peninsula to Carmel Beach is scenic and challenging. But scout from the shore first—rocky bluffs limit landing options until Stillwater Cove in Carmel (see Route 32: Stillwater.)

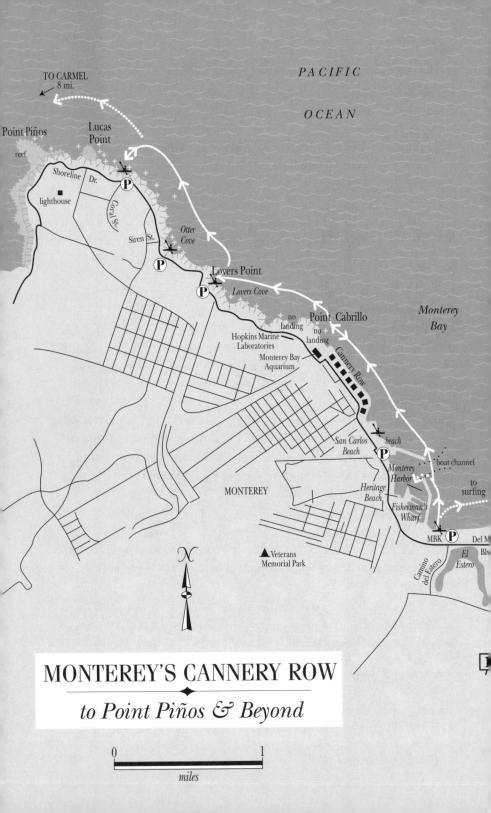

PACIFIC

OCEAN

TO CARMEL
8 mi.

Point Piños
reef

Lucas
Point

Shoreline Dr.

lighthouse

Coral St.

Siren St.

Otter
Cove

Lovers Point

Lovers Cove

no
landing

Point Cabrillo

no
landing

Monterey
Bay

Hopkins Marine
Laboratories

Monterey Bay
Aquarium

Cannery Row

San Carlos
Beach

beach

MONTEREY

Monterey
Harbor

boat channel

to
surfing

Heritage
Beach

Fisherman's
Wharf

N

MBK

Del M

Veterans
Memorial Park

Camino del Estero

El
Estero

Del
Blv

MONTEREY'S CANNERY ROW
◆
to Point Piños & Beyond

0   1

miles

Monterey Bay National Marine Sanctuary & the Submarine Canyon

Spanning one-fifth of the California coast and reaching between 10 and 50 miles out to sea, the Monterey Bay National Marine Sanctuary, the largest federally protected area outside Alaska, is the crown jewel of the marine sanctuary program. Among the most productive marine habitats on Earth, the sanctuary encompasses a "geographic convergence zone," an area of overlapping habitats where cold-water species from the north coexist with warm-water species from the south. Within its boundaries thrives a bounty of marine life: some two dozen marine mammals, including seals, otters, whales, and dolphins; nearly one hundred species of seabirds; and more than 300 species of fish. At the heart of the sanctuary, its raison d'ètre, is the Monterey Submarine Canyon, the deepest marine canyon on the West Coast of the lower 48. Twice the depth of the Grand Canyon, over 10,000 feet at its deepest point, the massive gorge cleaves Monterey Bay in two and reaches 60 miles into the Pacific. The sanctuary, with its access to abyssal depths so close to shore and its incredibly productive waters, offers unparalleled opportunity for marine research and a wildlife rich environment for paddling.

Where to Eat & Where to Stay

RESTAURANTS   **Grill on Lovers Point** (831–649–6859) at Lovers Beach makes a good en route lunch stop for burgers and sandwiches. Cannery Row and Fisherman's Wharf are loaded with restaurants.   **LODGING**   Accommodations also abound in this tourist mecca but may fill up on busy weekends. Near the launch site are **Del Monte Beach Inn** (831–649–4410) and **Fireside Lodge** (831–373–4172). Call the **Monterey Chamber of Commerce** (831–649–1770) for information. **CAMPING**   There are several private campgrounds in the area: **Veterans' Memorial Park** in Monterey (831–646–3865); **Saddle Mountain** in Carmel (831–624–1617); **Marina Dunes RV Park** in Marina (831–384–6914). (For state parks see Routes 26 and 30 Santa Cruz and Salinas River.)

Route 32:

----→

Stillwater Cove

This scenic pocket of shoreline within the Carmel Bay Ecological Reserve lies at the southern end of 17 Mile Drive, the exclusive community adjacent the world-famous Pebble Beach Golf Links. Although parking is restricted by number of vehicles and time of day, paddling here is worth the effort. A white sand beach surrounded by rocky outcrops within Stillwater Cove gives less-experienced paddlers an opportunity to meander in a generally protected area against a dramatic, open-coast backdrop. Longer, more challenging options are open to experienced kayakers.

TRIP HIGHLIGHTS: Scenery and wildlife: seals, otters, seabirds.

TRIP RATING:

Beginner: 1–2 miles within Stillwater Cove on days with no surf on the landing beach.

Intermediate: 3–5 miles for intermediates with previous coastal experience on days with swells below 4 feet and winds below 15 knots, especially if accompanied by an advanced leader. Good surfing at Carmel Beach in waves up to 3 feet. Protected rock gardens for skill building.

Advanced: 5 miles or more of open-coast touring along cliffs, often good on days when Point Lobos is too rough.

TRIP DURATION: Part or full day.

NAVIGATION AIDS: USGS *Monterey* (7.5 minute) and NOAA chart 18686. Wx radio: "Monterey Bay boaters' forecast"; buoys: Monterey and Point Piños.

TIDAL INFORMATION: Tide height has little effect.

CAUTIONS: Submerged rocks and surge within cove; offshore winds, boomers, cliffs, few landing options, and confused seas outside protection of cove.

TRIP PLANNING: Parking limited to six vehicles, so make reservations up to two weeks in advance by calling (831) 625–8507 —or take your chances. Time launching before 11:00 A.M. and after 2:00 P.M. when parking lot is closed to through traffic. Check weather radio on the Monterey side of Carmel Hill before you lose the signal.

LAUNCH SITE: The beach behind the Beach and Tennis Club is well protected, but parking can get crowded on weekends. From Highway 1 take the 17 Mile Drive/Highway 68 exit and follow signs to The Lodge at Pebble Beach and the Beach and Tennis Club (turn left on Palmetto Way, passing the lodge, and left again on Cypress Drive); pass the visitors' parking area at the 17th fairway and wind your way to the far end of the club's parking lot. After unloading your gear, park back at the visitors' lot. The 17 Mile Drive entrance fee is $7.25. There are public rest rooms. **Alternate launch sites:** The south end of Carmel Beach at the 8th Street stairs is more exposed and challenging.

DIRECTIONS

START: Launch from white sand beach to left of pier and head left along the shore.

MILE 0.5: **Arrowhead Point** makes a good turn-around spot, with good views of Carmel Bay. *Sidetrips:* On calm days the protected rock gardens inside the point make a good training area for intermediate paddlers, or you can round the point and land though small surf on the north end of Carmel Beach.

MILE 0.75: Check out the harbor seals resting on **Pescadero Rocks**, the rocky islets in the middle of the cove, while keeping your distance from them and submerged rocks.

MILE 1.0: Make a loop into the far end of the cove and out to **Pescadero Point**. *Caution:* The cliffy coastline beyond the point is scenic but exposed and has numerous offshore rocks. *Sidetrip:* Advanced paddlers can continue north 2 miles to Cypress Point, but landing possibilities are poor on rocky, pocket beaches along the cliffs. About 0.5 mile beyond Cypress Point is a sandy beach, but it's fully exposed to prevailing seas.

OTHER OPTIONS: On calm days intermediates can launch through small surf on Carmel Beach and paddle north into Stillwater. Advanced paddlers can round Monterey Peninsula from Point Piños. (See Route 31: Monterey/Cannery Row.)

Where to Eat & Where to Stay

RESTAURANTS There are many places to eat in Carmel. (See Routes 31 and 33: Monterey/Cannery Row and Point Lobos.) **LODGING** For a splurge try **The Lodge at Pebble Beach** or **The Inn at Spanish Bay** (both at 831–647–7500), where some suites cost as much as kayaks. (For less extravagant options see Route 31: Monterey/Cannery Row.) **CAMPING** (See Route 31: Monterey/Cannery Row.)

Stillwater Cove

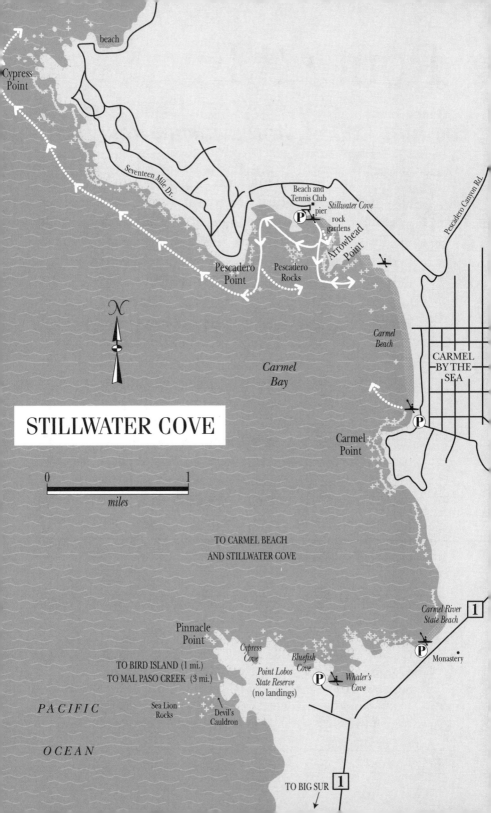

STILLWATER COVE

beach

Cypress
Point

Seventeen Mile Dr.

Pescadero Canyon Rd.

Beach and
Tennis Club
Stillwater Cove
pier
rock
gardens

Pescadero
Point

Pescadero
Rocks

Arrowhead
Point

Carmel
Beach

CARMEL
BY THE
SEA

N

Carmel
Bay

Carmel
Point

0   1
miles

TO CARMEL BEACH
AND STILLWATER COVE

Carmel River
State Beach

1

Pinnacle
Point

Cypress
Cove

Bluefish
Cove

TO BIRD ISLAND (1 mi.)
TO MAL PASO CREEK (3 mi.)

Point Lobos
State Reserve
(no landings)

Whaler's
Cove

Monastery

PACIFIC

Sea Lion
Rocks

Devil's
Cauldron

OCEAN

TO BIG SUR

1

Route 33:

------- ------- ------- ------- ------- ------- ------->

Point Lobos State Marine Reserve

With its abundant wildlife and quintessential Monterey scenery—postcard vistas of wind-sculpted cypress trees clinging to craggy granite cliffs—Point Lobos is one of our favorite coastal day trips. Sealife thrives amid thick kelp beds, the rainforests of the sea, enhanced by proximity to deep, nutrient rich water. Within 1 mile of shore, Carmel Canyon is 1,000 feet deep, dropping to 7,000 feet in just 6 miles where it joins the Monterey (submarine) Canyon off Point Piños. This sudden depth colors the seas an intense indigo blue and supports one of the richest ocean habitats in the world. Designated as the nation's first underwater reserve in 1960, the area is as sensitive as it is beautiful. It is a breeding area for harbor seals, sea lions, otters, and numerous seabird species, and unlike those in the well-traveled waters around Monterey, these animals remain wild and shy—requiring paddlers to maintain much greater distance to avoid disturbance. Named by early Spanish mariners for the constant barking of its *lobos del mar*, or "sea wolves," the point's vociferous colony of California sea lions flourishes to this day.

TRIP HIGHLIGHTS: World-class scenery and abundant wildlife.

TRIP RATING:

Beginner/Intermediate: 1–2 miles of safe harbor inside Whalers Cove on calm days if you stay well away from break zones at the cove edges and resist the urge to paddle out along the open coast. Strong intermediate paddlers may venture outside the coves on days with swells below 4 feet and winds below 15 knots, but it's strongly recommended that you do so with an advanced paddler leading.

Advanced: 4+ miles for experienced open-coast paddlers with strong water-reading skills and good sea sense. Excellent rock gardens, but swells above 8 feet limit access and make sightseeing difficult.

TRIP DURATION: Part or full day.

NAVIGATION AIDS: USGS *Monterey* (7.5 minute); the park map available for $1.00 at entrance station makes an excellent resource. Wx radio: "Monterey Bay boaters' forecast"; buoys: Monterey and Point Piños.

TIDAL INFORMATION: Tides have little effect except when extreme lows leave some rock gardens unrunnable.

CAUTIONS: Strong winds and submerged rocks and boomers abound, and cliffs prevent landing and create confused seas from rebounding swells. Extremely sensitive habitat for birds and seals, so landing is prohibited within the reserve except at Whalers for those with permits. Dumping shore break at Monastery Beach has earned it a reputation as a challenging launch site.

TRIP PLANNING: Pick your day; conditions are more enjoyable in swell below 6 feet, the calmer the better. Check weather radio on the Monterey side of Carmel Hill before you lose the signal.

LAUNCH SITE: For advanced paddlers, there is free parking at Monastery Beach (aka Carmel River State Beach) just outside the reserve on Highway 1, 2 miles south of Carmel. **Alternate launch site for beginners:** Launching from Whalers Cove inside the park requires a $6.00 entrance fee and a launch permit; permits sometimes available at front gate, but reservations are recommended through Park Net (800–444–7275). Limited to six boats per day.

DIRECTIONS

START: Launch from the more protected area on far southwest (left) corner of **Monastery Beach**. *Caution:* This is a difficult launch off a steep beach. Use teamwork to launch and if in doubt, don't go—the landing can be even worse, especially if the seas come up during the day as per usual. Stay outside the kelp beds, which get so thick and healthy that passing through them, you'll swear you're paddling through peanut butter.

MILE 1.0: **Whalers Cove** provides good protection for a rest, but the entrance isn't obvious until you are directly in front of it. *Caution:* To enter, swing wide and stay midchannel to avoid rocks. Landing is prohibited without a permit.

MILE 1.25: If seas are calm, pick your way through the rocks into **Bluefish Cove** for an up close look at some of the best scenery in the park. Keep a sharp eye out for seabirds, otters, and harbor seals, and keep your distance.

MILE 1.5: For expert paddlers several narrow channels around **Cypress Cove** are navigable on very calm days, some ending in long slots between cliffs barely wide enough to turn a kayak around. *Caution:* Paddling into these coves can be dangerous; large sneaker waves breaking over numerous submerged rocks and smashing against the cliffs can turn these coves from dead calm to deadly in a heartbeat.

Point Lobos State Marine Reserve

MILE 2.0: The west side of **Pinnacle Point**, which catches the full force of oceanic wind and swell, is a good turn-around point on rough days. *Sidetrips:* Continue south for a 5-mile, one-way trip to **Mal Paso Creek**. This sidetrip has an arduous landing, so be prepared for a long carry—and to scout the beach before you paddle, during some seasons and tide heights waves break on large boulders instead of sand. To reach Mal Paso you need to either paddle an extra 1 mile around the **Sea Lion Rocks** or take the shortcut through the infamous **Devils Cauldron**, which is often intense from waves rebounding between the cliffs and offshore rocks. The reward for continuing is more excellent rock gardens with small sea caves at the park's southern boundary, but stay well away from **Bird Island**, a sensitive breeding area for cormorants.

Where to Eat & Where to Stay

RESTAURANTS Many possibilities nearby in Carmel's Crossroads Shopping Center at Rio Road, including **R.G. Burgers** (831–626–8054), specializing in "Real Good" old-fashioned burgers, milkshakes, and vegetarian alternatives, and **Chevy's** (831–626–0945) Mexican food. **LODGING** (See Route 31: Monterey/Cannery Row.) **CAMPING** No camping facilities are available at Point Lobos. (See Route 31: Monterey/Cannery Row.)

Big Sur Coast to Morro Bay

Route 34:

Andrew Molera State Park
to Point Sur & Beyond

The very thing that makes paddling the Big Sur coast so difficult—its rugged inaccessibility—is precisely what makes it so appealing to some kayakers. If you can get your boat to the water, the paddling is excellent, but there are very few put ins—most of them are exposed to surf, rocky, and challenging. One exception is the sandy, protected beach at Andrew Molera. We should probably mention, however, that this exceptional beach is a full mile from the nearest parking lot. Anyone willing to carry a boat that far will be rewarded with the exceptional solitude and scenery this remote shoreline has to offer. Extensive kelp beds offshore are prime habitat for otters.

TRIP HIGHLIGHTS: Big Sur vistas, solitude, sea otters, rock gardens, and surfing.

TRIP RATING:

Intermediate: 1–6 miles for those with previous coastal paddling experience and an advanced paddler in the lead on day with no fog, surf below 3 feet, and wind below 15 knots.

Advanced: 1–6+ miles requiring strong water-reading skills. Because of numerous submerged rocks and boomers, we recommend following someone with previous local experience. Not recommended in swells above 6 feet, winds above 20–25 knots, or visibility less than 0.25 mile in fog.

TRIP DURATION: Part to full day.

NAVIGATION AIDS: USGS *Point Sur Quadrangle* (15 minute) and

NOAA chart 18686. Wx radio: "Pigeon Point to Point Piedras Blancas"; buoys: Point Piños, Point Piedras Blancas, and Cape San Martín.

TIDAL INFORMATION: More beaches available at low tide and more rocks exposed.

CAUTIONS: Highly exposed and remote. Thick fog in the morning and strong winds in the afternoon are common. A shallow shelf between Molera and Point Sur extends 1 mile from shore—its countless submerged rocks and reefy areas creating a minefield of boomers that can be challenging and fun on clear days with a low swell, but difficult and dangerous on foggy days with large swell. Sea otters and seals are common here and quite shy, so give them plenty of space.

TRIP PLANNING: Choose your day carefully: the calmer and clearer, the better for access to isolated beaches. Check your weather radio in Monterey or the Morro Bay area before the Santa Lucia Mountains block the signal. Bring kayak wheels for the 1-mile carry to the beach. Off the water, supplies and services are somewhat limited and pricey. Because the drive is awfully far for a day trip, we generally spend the night (or two) at Molera. Its first-come campground can get crowded on summer weekends but rarely fills, even on holidays. For other campgrounds or lodging, reserve well in advance.

LAUNCH SITE: From Highway 1, 3 miles north of Big Sur, turn into Andrew Molera State Park. Day-use fee; outhouses available. Walk-in campground is 0.5 mile down the trail toward the beach. From the campground it's another 0.5 mile to the beach. You might try bushwhacking your kayak to the creek and wading it down to the ocean if the current is slow. **Alternate launch sites:** Pfeiffer Beach—day-use fee, rest rooms, and limited parking.

DIRECTIONS

START: From **Molera Beach** paddle well around the rocks off the point and head north up the coast. *Caution:* There are submerged rocks and shallow reefs scattered along the entire stretch. *Sidetrip:* Head south around Cooper Point to Pfeiffer Beach. *Caution:* Scout carefully from

Andrew Molera State Park to Point Sur

Pfeiffer when you drop off the shuttle vehicle, this beach is rough and rocky *and conditions won't get any better as the day goes on.*

MILE 2.0: In the vicinity of **False Point Sur** are numerous isolated sandy beaches that will be yours alone if you can work your way to shore through the rocks. *Caution:* Private property on uplands, so stay on the beach.

MILE 3.0: The distinctive, 360-foot dome of **Point Sur**, one of the more prominent landmarks on the Central Coast, makes a good turn-around point most days. *Sidetrip:* On a calm day, more experienced paddlers may be able to round the point and continue another 2 miles to the beach at the mouth of the **Little Sur River** for possible landing. *Caution:* North side of Point Sur is extremely exposed, as are the beaches beyond. It is private property above high tide. Watch for steep shore break.

OTHER OPTIONS: On calm days it's possible to launch from **Pfeiffer Beach** and paddle up to Molera and back, avoiding the shuttle. There are also some nice beaches to the south of Pfeiffer Point, but if wind or fog comes up, getting back to Pfeiffer Beach can be extremely difficult or dangerous, and the next take out to the south at Limekiln Beach is nearly 30 miles away.

Where to Eat & Where to Stay

RESTAURANTS **River Inn Resort** (831–625–5255) at the north end of Big Sur has outdoor tables along the Big Sur River and live Dixieland jazz on Sunday afternoons. Next door, **Village Pub** (831–667–2355) serving great beer, pizza, and sandwiches, is one of the better values in the area. *Caution:* Expect any dining or accommodations in the Big Sur area to be more expensive than average. **LODGING** **River Inn** (800–548–3610) and **Big Sur Lodge** (800–4–Big Sur) offer the closest lodgings. There are cabins and camping at **Fernwood** (831–667–2422) and **Riverside Campground & Cabins** (831–667–2414). **CAMPING** Consider the two recommendations already mentioned and first-come, first-served walk-in sites at **Andrew Molera State Park** at the launch site, with outhouses but no showers. **Pfeiffer Big Sur State Park** has rest rooms with hot showers, takes reservations through Park Net (800–444–7275), and books months in advance.

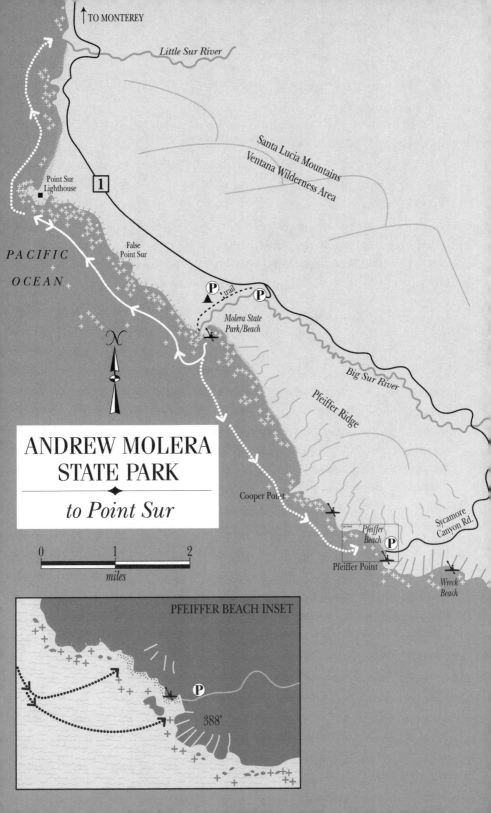

Big Sur Sea Otter Refuge

By the beginning of the twentieth century, after years of
intense hunting, sea otters were believed to be extinct on
the California coast. Their soft, luxurious pelts, which have
more hairs per square inch (up to a half million or more)
than any other animal, fetched hundreds of dollars each.
Ironically, one of the most efficient ways to hunt otters on
the open coast was by kayak, so greedy Russian fur traders
enslaved Aleutian islanders, perhaps the world's best ocean
kayakers, and systematically worked their way south.
Eventually joined by local Mexican and American hunters,
fur traders scoured the otters' West Coast range from
Alaska to Baja, finally "harvesting" every otter south of the
Canadian border. Or so they thought. During the
construction of Highway 1 to Big Sur in the 1930s, a raft of
otters was spotted. Apparently fifty or so had survived
among the massive kelp forests on this inaccessible stretch
of coast, and the area was designated a Sea Otter Game
Refuge. The current population of southern sea otter—
now numbering over 2,000 animals and stretching from San
Luis Obispo County to near San Francisco—all descends
from those wary few who had disappeared into rugged
folds of the Big Sur coast.

Route 35:

▬▬ ▬▬ ▬▬ ▬▬ ▬▬ ▬▬ ▬▬ ▬▬ ▬▬ ▬▬ ▬▬ ➤

Mill Creek to Lopez Point

This stretch of the Big Sur coast has two put ins within 3 miles of each other—places where you can drive to within a few yards of the beach—*and one of the sites has hot showers.* This may not seem like much to some paddlers, but in Big Sur these are amazing statements. The shoreline is rugged and wild as tectonic plates grind together, smashing pure rock straight up from the sea. Directly behind the launch sites towers Cone Peak, whose 5,155-foot summit plummets to the sea in just over 3 miles, making it the steepest coastal gradient in the lower 48. Along the entire 90-mile sweep of the Big Sur coast are perhaps a half dozen places to get your kayak to the water. The next launch sites to the north are an hour's drive distant: one is 1 mile from the parking lot; the other, rocky and exposed. The choices to the south, albeit closer, are nearly as bad. And here, in the lee of Lopez Point, lies close access to the beach—*twice*—one time with a shower.

TRIP HIGHLIGHTS: Access to the beach (with shower), Big Sur cliff hanging scenery, sea otters, seals, and seabirds.

TRIP RATING:
Intermediate: 1–10 miles for those with previous coastal paddling experience in waves below 3 feet and winds below 15 knots; helmets and surf zone skills required; advanced trip leader recommended.

Advanced: 1–10+ miles for experienced coastal kayakers; not recommended in seas above 6 feet and winds above 20 knots.

TRIP DURATION: Part to full day.

NAVIGATION AIDS: USGS *Lopez Point* and *Cape San Martín* (7.5 minute) and Forest Service map, *Los Padres National Forest.* Wx radio: "Pigeon Point to Point Piedras Blancas"; buoys: Point Piños, Cape San Martín, and Point Piedras Blancas.

TIDAL INFORMATION: Best selection of beaches at low tide. Beach access at Mill Creek hampered by tides above 3–4 feet.

CAUTIONS: Steep beaches with high degree of exposure, rocks, cliffs, boomers, morning fog, and afternoon wind.

TRIP PLANNING: Pick a day with midday low tide so beaches along the cliffs will be uncovered; scout carefully from the road for conditions on landing beaches en route. Check weather radio in Monterey or Morro Bay area before the mountains block the signal. Off the water services are limited: Both Lucia and Gorda have one minimart/gas station each with few supplies, short hours, and high prices. Campgrounds and lodgings are filled well in advance in summer. Hot showers are available at Limekiln even if you're not camping there ($3).

LAUNCH SITE: Mill Creek is 25 miles south of Big Sur on Highway 1, just past Kirk Creek Campground (4 miles south of Lucia). No fee, outhouse. **Alternate launch site:** Limekiln State Park (3 miles north of Mill Creek), day-use fee, rest rooms, and hot showers.

DIRECTIONS

START: From **Mill Creek** paddle out beyond rocks and kelp before heading to your right and up the coast.

MILE 1.0: Interspersed between rocky points are several small, sandy beaches along this stretch that make good rest stops at lower tide. *Caution:* Watch for submerged rocks in surf zone.

MILE 2.5: The sandy beach beneath the Highway 1 bridge at **Limekiln Creek State Park** is a good place to take a break; it offers rest rooms, picnic tables, and the best alternative launch site. *Caution:* This is a steep beach with dumping shore break; scout from shore first. *Sidetrip:* On very calm days, advanced paddlers can run the arch at the south end of Limekiln Beach. *Caution:* This arch can be extremely dangerous even in a moderate swell.

MILE 3.5: The steep, distinctive cliff of this minor headland has many seabird nests above and resembles Swiss cheese below with wave carved caves, crannies, and holes—none of them navigable. We've nicknamed

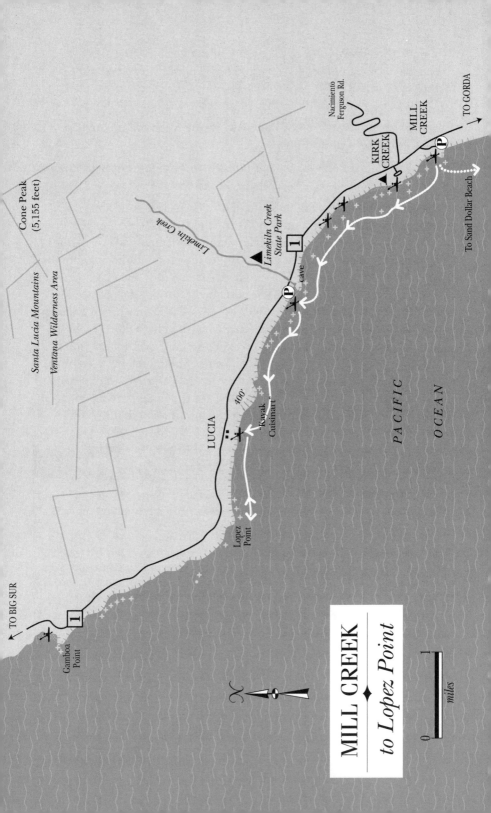

this cliff **"the kayak Cuisinart"** because of the curious way that waves washing into one opening sometimes spray, pour, and frappe out several other openings.

MILE 4.0: The handful of buildings on the cliff above is **Lucia**. On calm days careful landings are possible between the rocks on the small, steep beach at the base of the cliffs.

MILE 5.0: Lopez Point makes a good turn-around point with good views up the coast (but no beaches for several miles).

OTHER OPTIONS: The paddling south of Kirk Creek is as good as it gets, but beach access is not. Four miles south, the Sand Dollar Beach area has lovely sea stacks and a long sandy beach. However, only fanatics will deem the carry worth the effort: scaling the cliffs via stairway and switch-backing trail 0.5 mile to the parking lot. Three miles farther, Willow Creek is accessible only on calm days at low tide. The shoreline in front of the parking lot is boulder strewn. A sandy launch/landing beach is 0.25 mile over the slippery rocks to the north along a cliff face that is awash at high tide. The beach itself is steep with dumping shore break. Both Sand Dollar and Willow Creek are popular board surfing areas, which should tell you something of their exposure to waves. We've had more "adventures" and close calls here than we'd care to recall. It's no place for the timid or inexperienced. The next access is beyond Ragged Point, some 12 miles to the south.

Where to Eat & Where to Stay

R E S T A U R A N T S   Only two options unless you drive 45 minutes north to Big Sur (see rte. 34) and both are plain but pricey—it's a long way to the store, so expect to pay ten bucks for a burger. **Lucia Lodge** (831–667–2391) has a cafe and small store, or try the **Whale Watcher's Cafe** (801–927–1590) in Gorda. **L O D G I N G** **Lucia Lodge** (831–667–2391) has rustic cliff-side cottages. (See Route 34: Molera for other options.)   **C A M P I N G**   There is camping at **Kirk Creek** and 5 miles south at **Plaskett Creek**, but these Forest Service campsites are "first come, first served"; don't expect to get a campsite on summer weekends if you arrive after 10:00 A.M. on Friday. **Limekiln State Park** takes reservations through Park Net (800–444–7275) and fills months in advance. (See rte. 34.)

A Glimpse of the Real Big Sur

Much more than the scattering of restaurants, art galleries, and inns that hug Highway 1 in "town," Big Sur is like the name given it by the original Spanish settlers in Monterey—*el Sur Grande*—that big place to the south, which stretches from Carmel to San Simeon, encompassing the coastal mountains and all of the Ventana Wilderness Area. More than anything, perhaps, it is these mountains, the Santa Lucia Range, and their proximity to the sea, that *makes* Big Sur. The range is not particularly high, topping out at just under 6,000 feet, but what it lacks in stature is made up for in steepness. Driven by a collision of tectonic plates, the main ridge of the Santa Lucias surges straight from the sea like a monster wave to over 3,000 feet. This relatively young range, which was near sea level just 2 million years ago (a quick tick on the geologic clock), is still on the rise at an average of a foot or two every thousand years. When the ocean gets rough, the full force of Pacific swells batters the seawall cliffs, sculpting them into craggy coves, carving out sea caves, and scattering a debris of rock gardens at their feet. This dynamic blend of water and rock creates some of the most celebrated coastal scenery on Earth, with some 3 million visitors overlooking these grand vistas each year. Yet very few get the chance to see this famous meeting of land and sea from water level, and there's nothing quite like a seal's eye view, with salt spray light on your skin and the rumble of waves against cliffs echoing in your ears.

Route 36:

━━ ━━ ━━ ━━ ━━ ━━ ━━ ━━ ━━ ━━ ━━ ━━ ▶

San Simeon Bay & Beyond

It was no mistake when William Randolph Hearst chose this picturesque cove as the site for his "beach bungalow" below Hearst Castle. This beautiful and protected white sand beach makes a classic scene and a fine backdrop for coastal touring. On calm days beginners can explore along the cliffs within the cove, and more experienced kayakers have excellent access to open-coast rock gardens and isolated beaches. Sea otters and seals are common in the area, as are fine coastal vistas. At the base of the Big Sur coast, this area retains a similar "wild" feel without the same exposure.

TRIP HIGHLIGHTS: Scenery, protected coastal paddling, access to isolated beaches, otters, seals, and seabirds.

TRIP RATING:

Beginner: 1–2 miles in lee of San Simeon Point on days with less than 1 foot surf on beach and winds below 10–15 knots; company of experienced partner recommended.

Intermediate: 1–4 miles on day with less than 3-foot surf and 15 knots wind, best to go on a fogless day, and advanced partner recommended beyond San Simeon Point.

Advanced: 4+ miles with access to rock gardens and surf.

TRIP DURATION: Part to full day.

NAVIGATION AIDS: USGS *San Simeon* (7.5 minute). Wx radio: "Piedras Blancas to Point Arguello"; buoys: Point Piedras Blancas, Diablo Canyon, and Port San Luis.

TIDAL INFORMATION: More beaches but more rocks at lower tides.

CAUTIONS: Surf, rocks, wind, and fog.

TRIP PLANNING: Better beach access at tides below 4 feet. Paddle early before wind, especially if rounding San Simeon Point.

LAUNCH SITE: Turn west off Highway 1 into William Randolph Hearst State Beach, directly across from the turn off to Hearst Castle. Park in lower lot to right of fishing pier. Use fee is $3.00 per day. Rest rooms and cold showers available. **Alternate launch sites:** beach 3 miles north at Arroyo Laguna or 7 miles north at beach on north side of Piedras Blancas Motel; parking free, facilities at motel.

DIRECTIONS

START: Launch to **right of pier near creek mouth** and head right, paralleling the curve of shore. *Sidetrip:* Head left around pier to fine rock gardens beginning 0.5 mile to south. *Caution:* Avoid harbor seals hauled out on offshore rocks.

MILE 0.5: **Bluffs** begin at end of sandy beach. This is the most protected end of the beach and a nice place for a picnic or to practice surf landings.

MILE 1.0: Continue contouring along the bluffs to scenic **San Simeon Point**, thickly forested in cypress and eucalyptus. A small beach just inside the point makes a great private lunch stop if tide and swell permit (at low tide rocks choke the narrow entrance, and at high tide the beach may be awash). *Caution:* Submerged rocks extend well out beyond the point. Swing wide if you continue along the exposed, rocky shoreline beyond.

MILE 2.0: Follow the cliffs past several rocky, exposed pocket beaches (accessible only at low tide and swell) to the **protected cove** in the lee of the next point. The best landing is in far left corner on steep but protected beach that may be awash during higher tides and swells. *Sidetrip:* Continue north another 1.5 miles to beach at Arroyo Laguna.

OTHER OPTIONS: Run shuttle and paddle south 7 miles one way from Piedras Blancas Motel or 3.5 miles from Arroyo Laguna. *Caution:* Elephant seal colonies claim many of the good landing beaches between Piedras Blancas and Arroyo Laguna, so landing may not be possible. To the south, paddle 5 miles one way to San Simeon Beach State Park. Scout all landings carefully from the shore first.

San Simeon Bay

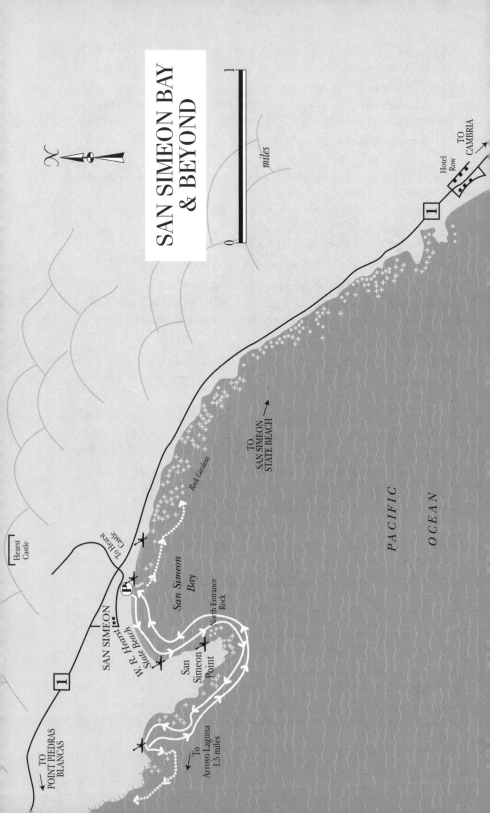

SAN SIMEON BAY
& BEYOND

miles

0   1

TO
POINT PIEDRAS
BLANCAS

Hearst
Castle

SAN SIMEON

To Hearst
Castle

W. R. Hearst
State Beach

Rock Gardens

San Simeon
Bay

San
Simeon
Point

North Entrance Rock

To
Arroyo Laguna
1.5 miles

TO
SAN SIMEON
STATE BEACH

PACIFIC

OCEAN

Hotel
Row

TO
CAMBRIA

Where to Eat & Where to Stay

RESTAURANTS   Small snack bar at Hearst Beach sells prepackaged sandwiches and frozen burritos, but better choices can be had down the street at **Sebastian's Patio Cafe** (805–927–4217) (fish and chips, burgers, etc.) or 3 miles south on Highway 1 along "hotel row" in San Simeon.   **LODGING**   **Piedras Blancas Motel** (805–927–4202) has rustic bungalows on bluffs; many other options are found 3 miles south along "hotel row" in San Simeon or 7 miles south in Cambria.   **CAMPING**   **San Simeon Beach State Park**, 5 miles south on Highway 1, has hot showers; make reservations through Park Net (800–444–7275). (Also see Route 38: Morro Bay.)

Route 37:

▬ ▬ ▬ ▬ ▬ ▬ ▬ ▬ ▬ ▬ ▬ ▬ ▬ ▬ ➤

Cayucos State Beach to Point Estero

In the lee of Point Estero, the shoreline faces south for half a dozen miles, forming good shelter from prevailing wind and swell. The point's steep cliffs give way to low bluffs, backed by a coastal bench or *marine terrace* (see page 193). In front of this terrace, a second shallow platform extends well out to sea, forming an outer reef that absorbs the brunt of the waves and leaves a jigsaw puzzle of rocks scattered across the more protected inner waters. This coincidence of southern exposure and shallow, rocky shelf creates one of the more extensive *and most accessible* rock garden areas in Central California. On calm days this area provides an excellent introduction to the fun of rock garden exploration, but there's still more to recommend it. Sea otters and seals frequent these waters. Along shore, many pocket beaches dot the bluffs. Because the grassy cow pasture behind the bluffs is private property, these beaches feel quite remote and isolated, despite the proximity of Highway 1. The highway cannot be seen from the beach, but it is nonetheless accessible in case of emergency, adding a margin of safety.

TRIP HIGHLIGHTS: Excellent introductory rock gardens, secluded beaches, scenery, and an excellent place to see otters and seals.

TRIP RATING:

Beginner: 1–2 miles on days with 1 foot surf on the beach, less than 10 knots of wind; not recommended going beyond immediate beach area without an experienced paddler leading (tours available through Good Clean Fun [805–995–1993] on Front Street).

Intermediate: 1–4 miles on days with less than 3-foot surf on beach and 15 knots wind for those with previous coastal paddling experience or with an advanced trip leader.

Advanced: 1–11+ miles of excellent rock garden and surf play in waves to 6 feet and winds to 20 knots.

TRIP DURATION: Part to full day.

NAVIGATION AIDS: USGS *Cayucos* (7.5 minute) and NOAA chart 18703. Wx radio: "Piedras Blancas to Point Arguello"; buoys: Point Piedras Blancas, Diablo Canyon, and Port San Luis.

TIDAL INFORMATION: Better beach access and better protection in rock gardens during lower tides.

CAUTIONS: Surf, rocks, boomers, wind, fog, seal haul outs, and private property above beaches.

TRIP PLANNING: Paddle early before wind, especially if rounding Cayucos Point. A day with low tide in late morning would give best protection from both wind and swell in the rock gardens. Avoid paddling in thick fog; rocks and shore will be difficult to spot.

LAUNCH SITE: Sandy, gently sloping Cayucos State Beach provides a fairly well-protected launch through small to moderate surf. Take Cayucos Drive off Highway 1, turn right on North Ocean Avenue, then an immediate left into the parking lot on the north side of the pier. Free parking, rest rooms, and cold showers. **Alternate launch sites:** Beach on north end of Studio Drive, 2 miles to the south has less protection but is a more scenic spot to launch on calm days; parking free, no facilities.

DIRECTIONS

START: Launch on the right near the mouth of **Cayucos Creek,** swinging wide to avoid the submerged rocks around the point to the right. *Sidetrip:* In the cove just beyond the point is the beginning of the "inside passage": an excellent rock garden playground for the next 2 miles with good protection during low tide and swell. There are many small, private beaches if you can work your way through the rocks. *Caution:* boomers, waves breaking into rocks, seal haul outs, and private property above beaches.

Cayucos State Beach to Point Estero

MILE 2.0: Exposure gradually increases as you approach **Cayucos Point**. Good landing at **Byron's Beach** (by the windmill) makes a good turn-around spot for most paddlers on most days. *Caution:* Advanced paddlers (or trip leaders) are strongly recommended because exposure increases beyond Cayucos Point. Here numerous reefs and seal haul outs force you well out to sea for an exposed rounding of the outer reef, where waves may break 0.5 mile or more offshore.

MILE 3.0: Sandy beach in the cove just north of the point gets good protection from the reef. *Sidetrip:* Although more exposed here, the "inside passage" continues with more advanced rock garden play for the next 1 mile and more small beaches.

MILE 4.0: The wide beach where the bluffs end at the mouth of **Villa Creek** makes a better landmark (it's the only beach that big) than a landing. Not that anything's wrong with this beach, but it's not as pretty or private as the "pocket" beaches you've been passing, and there are no bluffs for wind protection.

MILE 5.5: Cliffs steepen and rock gardens and landing beaches give out during this last 1.5 miles to **China Harbor**. The beach here is very remote and private.

OTHER OPTIONS: The 6-mile, one-way trip from Cayucos to Morro Bay makes a dramatic entrance to the harbor with great views of Morro Rock.

Where to Eat & Where to Stay

R E S T A U R A N T S Several restaurants can be found along the beach front in Cayucos, and have take-out menus featuring fresh local fish and chips, or try **Schooner's Wharf** (805–995–3883), which has higher-end dining with steaks and seafood. **L O D G I N G** **Shoreline Inn** (805–995–6381) is one of several beach front hotels on North Ocean Street. **C A M P I N G** See Route 38: Morro Bay.

Cayucos State Beach to Point Estero

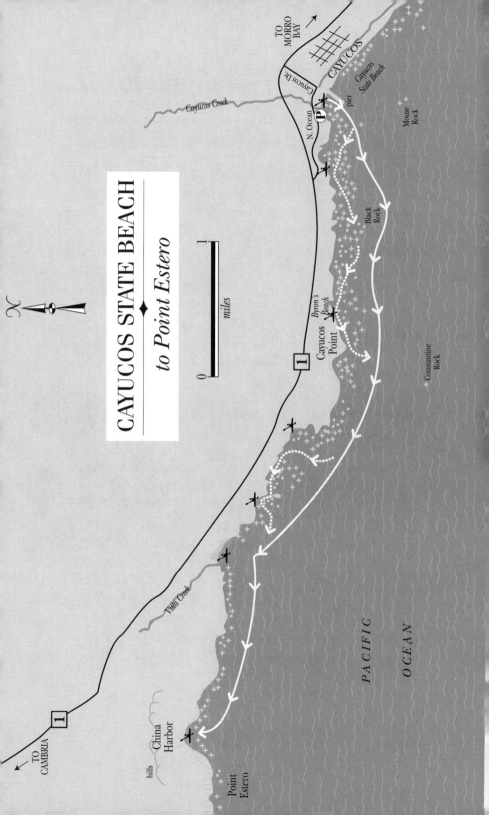

Wavecut Platforms & Marine Terraces

Big waves crashing against rocks can produce pressures greater than 1,000 pounds per square foot. In areas where sedimentary rock forms the shore, this constant gnawing of surf erodes the California coast at an average of six to twelve inches each year, over time creating wide, gently sloping benches called *wavecut platforms*. Over the past few million years, uplifting along the West Coast has gradually raised the shoreline, stranding ancient wavecut platforms well above sea level. These familiar coastal benchlands are termed *marine terraces* by geologists. The state's more extensive marine terraces were carved as sea level rose during interglacial periods, and today's wavecut platforms began forming some seventeen thousand years ago with our current rise in sea level.

Route 38:

```
■ ■ ■ ■ ■ ■ ■ ■ ■ ■ ■ ■ ■ ■ ■ ➤
```

Morro Bay Estuary

The sheltered estuary at Morro Bay, bordered by nature preserves, is prime habitat for beginning paddlers, as few areas provide such sealife, scenery, and solitude so close at hand. The largest coastal wetlands in the area south of Elkhorn Slough, the bay, which encompasses the fertile salt marsh of Morro Estuary Natural Preserve, is among the West Coast's better birding spots. Over 250 species have been recorded in the area with winter migrants flocking in by the tens of thousands. Paddlers also see harbor seals, sea lions, and otters, and, after a short crossing to the sandspit in Morro Dunes Natural Preserve, they are treated to remote beach hiking with great ocean views. Options abound for beginners, and the bay is also a good spot to build intermediate skills in a fairly protected setting.

TRIP HIGHLIGHTS: Excellent birding, scenery, and hiking.

TRIP RATING:

Beginner: 4–5 mile loop to mouth and back. Basic knowledge of tides and boat traffic rules a must. For shorter trips of 2 to 3 miles, cross to the sandspit for a hike or explore the marsh at the mouth of Osos Creek.

Intermediate: Practice ferrying in currents at the end of the sandspit or try surfing inside the jetty on days when waves are less than 3 feet.

Advanced: (See Route 39: Morro Rock to Spooners Cove/Montaña de Oro.)

TRIP DURATION: Part or full day.

NAVIGATION AIDS: USGS *Morro Bay South* (7.5 minute) and NOAA chart 18703. Wx radio: "Piedras Blancas to Point Arguello"; buoys: Point Piedras Blancas, Diablo Canyon, and Port San Luis.

TIDAL INFORMATION: Extensive mudflats begin to uncover at tides below 2 or 3 feet, but a boat channel along the near (eastern) shore keeps the bay navigable to Baywood Park at any water level.

CAUTIONS: Mudflats, afternoon winds, boat traffic around main harbor area, tidal currents and rips at the mouth of the bay, and breaking waves at ocean jetties.

TRIP PLANNING: If crossing to the sandspit, novices should paddle early before the wind kicks up. Pick a day with a rising tide to avoid getting stuck in the muck. When returning from the mouth, the longer you wait after high tide, the more mud and opposing current you'll have to fight.

LAUNCH SITE: The beach north of the Museum of Natural History provides easy access, but it can be muddy at low tide. From Highway 1 take the Los Osos/Baywood exit onto South Bay

Boulevard. Following the signs to Morro Bay State Park, turn right on State Park Road, pass the park entrance, and go to the first beach after the museum. Free parking. Facilities are in the state park. **Alternate launch sites:** Marina across from state park entrance and boat ramp at end of the Embarcadero are less muddy at low tide; Coleman Park is good for paddling near the mouth (see rte. 39); in Baywood Park try the end of Santa Ysabel Road. Free parking at all sites.

DIRECTIONS

START: From launch beach head west to the dunes, staying left of **Grass Island** and its seal haul out. To hike across the sandspit, aim for the saddle on the dunes at 250° (mag.). *Sidetrips:* The eucalyptus grove on **Fairbank Point**, a quarter mile north of the launch site, shelters one of California's largest great blue heron rookeries. From early spring through early summer, herons and egrets nest here. Interested birders can swing by the rookery before crossing the bay, or they can avoid crossing the bay and follow the shoreline south at high tide for 2 miles into the narrowing channels of **Morro Estuary Natural Preserve** for some of the area's best birdwatching.

MILE 1.0: On reaching the **sand spit,** paddle north along it. *Sidetrip:* Head south into the back bay for more solitude (if you've considered the effects of wind and tides on your return).

MILE 1.5: As the **dunes** recede the hike across for an ocean view gets slightly shorter.

MILE 2.5: Great view of **Morro Rock** from the end of the spit and a good spot for a rest before heading back along the waterfront. *Caution:* Currents, waves, and boat traffic can cause hazardous conditions in the channel at the end of the spit.

MILE 3.0: Morro Bay's **Embarcadero** is a picturesque, New England–style waterfront replete with a working fishing fleet and a plethora of small gift shops and restaurants. Landings are permitted on two small, public dingy docks, one across from the **#12 channel marker** on the north side of the Galley Restaurant, and the other farther down at the Fish Bowl. *Caution:* Avoid boat traffic by skirting the right (west) side of the boat lane outside the channel markers.

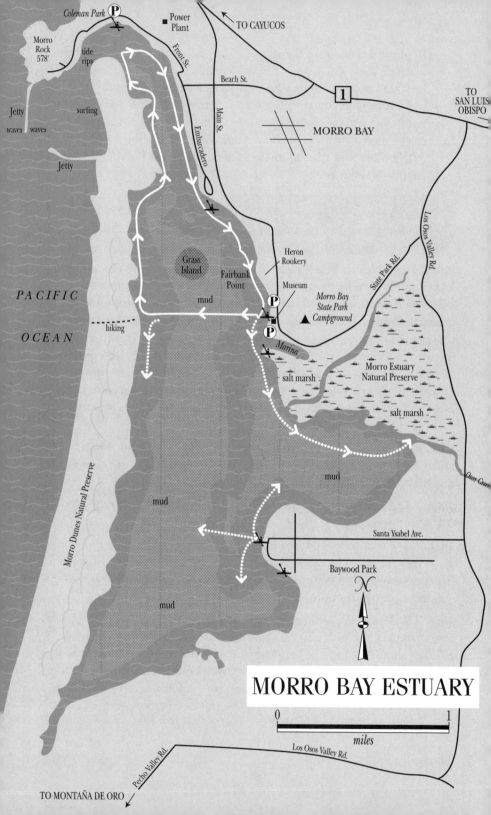

Coleman Park **P**

■ Power Plant

TO CAYUCOS

Morro Rock 578'

tide rips

Front St.

Beach St.

1

TO SAN LUIS OBISPO

Jetty

surfing

waves waves

Jetty

Main St.

Embarcadero

MORRO BAY

PACIFIC

OCEAN

hiking

Grass Island

mud

Fairbank Point

Heron Rookery

Museum

P

P

Marina

salt marsh

Los Osos Valley Rd.

State Park Rd.

Morro Bay State Park Campground

Morro Estuary Natural Preserve

salt marsh

Osos Creek

Morro Dunes Natural Preserve

mud

mud

mud

mud

Santa Ysabel Ave.

Baywood Park

N

MORRO BAY ESTUARY

0   1

miles

Los Osos Valley Rd.

Pecho Valley Rd.

TO MONTAÑA DE ORO

Morro Rock
and the Seven Sisters

One of the more prominent coastal landmarks in the state, 578-foot Morro Rock is the last of the Seven Sisters, a series of dramatic outcrops (there are nine actually), stretching over 10 miles inland in a line to San Luis Obispo. The word *morro*, Spanish for a dome-shaped promontory, accurately reflects the distinctive shape of this peak, which has for centuries been an important landmark for mariners. It's believed that volcanic activity some 20 million years ago formed this row of peaks, which have since been eroded to their stony cores. Once quarried, Morro Rock is now protected as both a Registered Historical Landmark and a nature preserve. And as appealing as it may look to climbers, scaling the peak is illegal and dangerous.

Where to Eat & Where to Stay

RESTAURANTS   Feeding options abound along the Embarcadero, from fresh local seafood at the **Fish Bowl** (805–772–3324) to cappuccino, ice cream, and salt water taffy.   **LODGING**   Lodging is plentiful, especially along Main Street, two blocks from water; for information call the Morro Bay Chamber of Commerce (805–772–4467). **The Back Bay Inn** in Baywood Park (805–528–1233) offers casual accommodations in a quiet, waterfront location with launching access for guests. **CAMPING**   **Morro Bay State Park** has camping with hookups and hot showers. **Morro Strand State Beach** 2 miles north on Highway 1 has beachfront camping but only cold, outdoor showers. **Montaña de Oro State Park** south of Los Osos is more scenic and primitive with outhouses and water, but no showers or hookups. Call Park Net for reservations (800–444–7275).

Route 39:

![arrow](dashed arrow)

Morro Rock to Spooners Cove in Montaña de Oro

The dynamic stretch of uninhabited coastline south of Morro Rock offers some of the more dramatic scenery and challenging conditions in the area. Leaving the protection of Morro Bay reveals spectacular views of Morro Rock's steep ocean side and the cliffs along Montaña de Oro State Park—the "Mountain of Gold" coined by Spanish explorers for the California poppies and other wildflowers that blanket its bluffs each spring.

TRIP HIGHLIGHTS: Outstanding coastal vistas, surfing, and solitude.

TRIP RATING:

Intermediate: Because of its exposure, we only recommend this trip to intermediates with previous open-coast experience, preferably led by an advanced paddler on a calm day with waves below 4 feet and winds to 15 knots. Good surf zone practice between south jetties, but beware of getting swept out to sea during strong ebb tides.

Advanced: The 7-mile, one-way trip suggested here requires a shuttle; to avoid shuttling (or to shorten or lengthen the mileage), launch from Spooners and paddle north toward Morro Bay for whatever distance, then return with the afternoon wind for a round-trip of up to 14 miles. Good surfing can be found all along the sandspit in waves to 6 feet or so, and we've even managed to run this trip in swells over 12 feet (not recommended) by staying well out to sea. For expert paddlers the 12-mile roadless stretch from Spooners to Port San Luis is among the more challenging and rewarding trips on the West Coast.

TRIP DURATION: Part to full day.

NAVIGATION AIDS: USGS *Morro Bay South* (7.5 minute) and NOAA chart 18703. Wx radio: "Piedras Blancas to Point Arguello"; buoys: Point Piedras Blancas, Diablo Canyon, and Port San Luis.

TIDAL INFORMATION: Tide height makes little difference along most of this stretch, but more landing beaches and more rocks are exposed along the cliffs during lower tides.

CAUTIONS: Conditions can change quickly here as the warning sign at the harbor mouth would suggest: HAZARDOUS WATER AHEAD— OFTEN UNSAFE FOR SMALL CRAFT. This trip runs the gamut of coastal hazards: boat traffic, tide rips, breaking waves, strong afternoon winds, fog, and surf—*and that's just leaving the harbor mouth.* On the open coast submerged rocks and sneaker waves can appear up to 0.5 mile from shore during a big swell. The steep, gravel beach at Spooners can look deceptively calm between sets of hard-dumping shore break.

TRIP PLANNING: Scout first to assess conditions before leaving the shelter of Morro Bay. Where the road dead ends at Morro Rock provides a good place to get a look at sea conditions, as do the bluffs above Spooners Cove at the take out.

LAUNCH SITE: From Highway 1 take the Main Street exit into Morro Bay, turn right on Beach Street, right again onto Front Street, and then follow the waterfront past the power plant to Coleman Park, where Coleman Drive heads out to Morro Rock. Launch from the small access beach across from park entrance. Free parking. **Alternate launch sites:** Try up the coast at Morro Strand or Cayucos State Beach (see Route 38: Morro Bay for more on launch sites). Landing site: Spooners Cove at Montaña de Oro State Park has free parking for your shuttle vehicle. From Highway 1 south of Morro Bay, take the Los Osos/Baywood exit onto South Bay Boulevard, following the signs to Montaña de Oro. Turn right on Los Osos Valley Road and follow it into the park (where it becomes Pecho Valley Road). The dirt lot at Spooners is on the right just before park headquarters

START: From the beach on Jetty Road, head out the mouth past **Morro Rock**. *Caution:* tide rips, breaking waves, and boat traffic.

MILE 1.0: When you reach the open sea, reassess conditions because it won't get any calmer as the day progresses. *Caution:* Stay well beyond the breakers and head south along shore; when a big swell is running, sneaker waves can break well out to sea. *Sidetrips:* Good surfing can often be had at the semiprotected beach between the south jetties. This makes a fun day trip for paddlers who are crunched for time or feeling less ambitious about running a shuttle to Montaña de Oro. Or you can paddle north along the back side of Morro Rock for dramatic views of the cliffs, often with pounding surf and nesting seabirds. Expect confused seas with lots of rebound and chop.

MILE 2.0: If you have strong surf zone skills and a calm day, you may land anywhere along the sandspit from here to where the bluffs begin around mile 4.5.

MILE 4.5: Once the bluffs begin landings are difficult or impossible from here to Spooners, except for a few steep, low-tide pocket beaches against the cliffs.

MILE 6.0: The narrow gully backed by a eucalyptus grove on the otherwise treeless bluffs is **Hazard Canyon**. Landing may be possible or just use it as a landmark—it's halfway down the bluffs to Spooners. *Caution:* If landing, stay several hundred yards to the left (north) side of the beach and away from **Hazard Reef**, which extends 0.25 mile or more from the mouth of the gully.

MILE 7.0: The first obvious point along this fairly straight shoreline marks the far side of **Spooners Cove**. Look for cars parked along the bluffs, hikers, and, if it's not foggy, the distinctive cone-shape of **Valencia Peak**, which dominates the ridgeline behind the take out. *Caution:* Don't cut the corner when landing; swing wide, staying to the deep water midchannel to avoid submerged rocks on the left (north) side. The landing itself is well protected but steep, sometimes there is a strong surge or dumping shore break.

Where to Eat & Where to Stay

See Route 38: Morro Bay for information on restaurants, lodging, and camping.

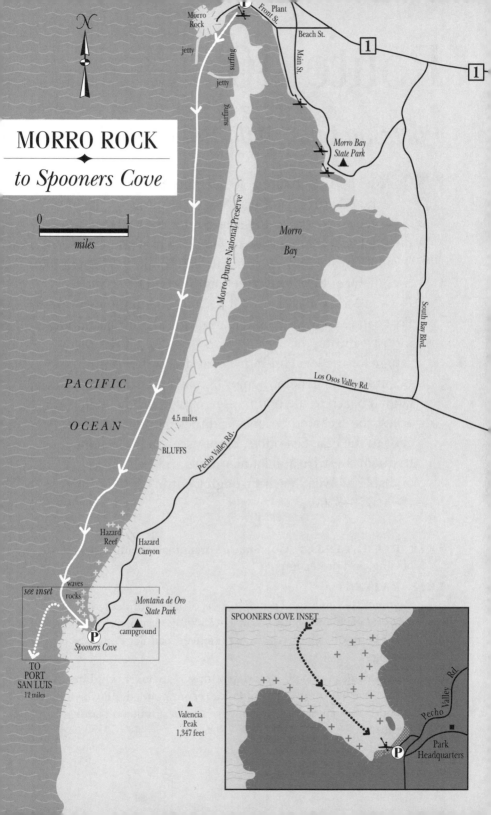

MORRO ROCK

to Spooners Cove

N

0   1
miles

PACIFIC

OCEAN

Morro Rock

jetty

surfing

jetty

surfing

Plant

Front St.

Beach St.

Main St.

1

1

Morro Bay State Park

Morro Bay

Morro Dunes National Preserve

South Bay Blvd.

Los Osos Valley Rd.

4.5 miles

BLUFFS

Pecho Valley Rd.

Hazard Reef

Hazard Canyon

waves

rocks

see inset

Montaña de Oro State Park

campground

Spooners Cove

TO PORT SAN LUIS
12 miles

Valencia Peak
1,347 feet

SPOONERS COVE INSET

Pecho Valley Rd.

Park Headquarters

Route 40:

━━ ━━ ━━ ━━ ━━ ━━ ━━ ━━ ━━ ━━ ━━ ━━ ➤

Port San Luis, Avila Beach, & Beyond

Tucked in the substantial lee of Point San Luis, the sheltered arc of San Luis Obispo Bay provides the most protected coastal touring for a hundred miles in either direction. To augment the bay's excellent natural shelter, a 0.5-mile breakwater was constructed around the turn of the twentieth century from materials quarried from Morro Rock in Morro Bay (before it became a nature preserve). Port San Luis provided safe harbor for a thriving shipping industry during the last 150 years or so, and it is now a refuge for the local fishing fleet and a few kayakers. Beginners will generally enjoy flatwater all the way from the launch beach to the point; more experienced paddlers can access the secluded beaches and rock gardens along the cliffs to the east. Sea otters, harbor seals, and sea lions frequent the area, and kayak rentals and tours are available at Avila Beach through Central Coast Kayaks; (805) 773–3500.

TRIP HIGHLIGHTS: Good marine mammal viewing, ocean birding, and protection.

TRIP RATING:

Beginner: 1–3 miles to Point San Luis on days with less than 1-foot surf on beach and winds below 10–15 knots. May head south of Fossil Point on calm day with experienced paddler (with tow rope) leading.

Intermediate: 1–5+ miles on days with surf to 3 feet, winds to 15 knots. Beaches south of Fossil Point recommended only for those with previous coastal touring experience or advanced paddler in the lead.

Advanced: 1–5+ miles with access to rock gardens and isolated beaches.

TRIP DURATION: Part to full day.

NAVIGATION AIDS: USGS *Port San Luis and Pismo Beach* (7.5 minute) and NOAA chart 18703. Wx radio: "Point Piedras Blancas to Point Arguello"; buoys: Port San Luis, Point Piedras Blancas, and Diablo Canyon.

TIDAL INFORMATION: Little effect except extreme high tides may cover some beaches.

CAUTIONS: Offshore wind, surf, rocks, boat traffic, fog, and seal haul outs.

TRIP PLANNING: Paddle early before wind or hug shore to stay in wind shadow of San Luis Hill.

LAUNCH SITE: To reach Olde Port Beach Launching Access from Highway 101, take Avila Beach exit west and follow signs toward Port San Luis on Avila Beach Drive. Pass Avila Beach and look for launch beach on left just beyond the long, white pier. Free parking, rest rooms. **Alternate launch site:** Far west end of Avila Beach near creek and away from swimmers.

DIRECTIONS

START: Launch from sandy beach at **Olde Port Launching Access** and head right, contouring along bluffs. *Sidetrip:* Head south to Avila Beach (landing permitted only on far west side near San Luis Creek) or 2 miles beyond to Pirates Cove (see Other Options).

MILE 0.75: Once you reach the steeper terrain behind **Harford Pier**, the last canopied pier in the state, you should enjoy excellent wind protection. Round the pier or paddle carefully under it, avoiding any fishing lines.

MILE 1.5: The beach at the base of the jetty just past **Smith Island** is fairly isolated, offering good views up the coast. It is well protected and should make an easy landing in all but the highest tides. This is a good place to turn around, especially if it's windy. *Caution:* Stay close to shore if the wind has come up. The farther you stray from the wind shadow of San Luis Hill, the harder the wind blows *offshore.*

MILE 2.0: For more experienced paddlers, paddling to the end of the **breakwater** provides a good view of sea lions hauled out on the jetty and excellent vistas of the wild coastline to the north. *Caution:* If the wind is blowing, the return along the jetty can be difficult. Wind blows offshore, and if you aren't strong enough to fight it, your next landfall is somewhere around Pismo Beach, across 5 miles or so of open ocean. Extreme exposure and no landing beaches for several miles north of Point San Luis.

OTHER OPTIONS: On calm days experienced paddlers can explore the cliffs, coves, and rock gardens between Fossil Point and Pirates Cove. *Caution:* Returning to Avila against the afternoon wind can be difficult. Also, note that the pretty, secluded beach at Pirates Cove is "clothing optional."

Where to Eat & Where to Stay

RESTAURANTS Several restaurants along Avila's quaint 3-block-long beachfront feature locally caught seafood, chowder, and fish and chips, including the **Old Custom House** (805–595–7555), which has a casual atmosphere and a patio sun deck, and **Jetty Restaurant** (805–595–2929). **LODGING** The **Inn at Avila Beach** (805–595–2300) overlooks the ocean at the east end of the beach. A few miles inland, **Sycamore Mineral Springs** has rooms with private outdoor hot tubs. Tub rentals also available by the hour for an aprés-paddle soak. The setting is very romantic as the secluded tubs are scattered beneath the oaks on a steep hillside (800–234–5831). **CAMPING** (See Route 38: Morro Bay.)

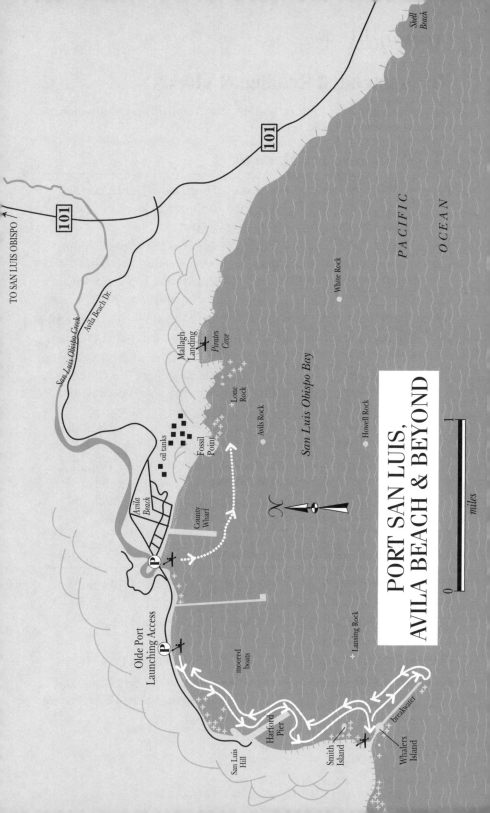

TO SAN LUIS OBISPO

101

101

San Luis Obispo Creek

Avila Beach Dr.

Mallagh Landing

Pirates Cove

oil tanks

Fossil Point

Avila Beach

County Wharf

Lone Rock

Avils Rock

White Rock

PACIFIC OCEAN

San Luis Obispo Bay

Howell Rock

Olde Port Launching Access

moored boats

San Luis Hill

Hartford Pier

Smith Island

Lansing Rock

Whalers Island

breakwater

miles

0 1

PORT SAN LUIS,
AVILA BEACH & BEYOND

Shell Beach

Appendix A

Recommended Reading & Videos

The following titles are our response to the frequently asked question,
"What books or videos do you recommend?"

Classic Instruction Manuals

Bascom, Williard, *Waves and Beaches* (Anchor Books Doubleday &
Company, Inc., 1990). More than you need to know on the topic,
but an excellent oceanography reference.

Burch, David, *Fundamentals of Kayak Navigation* (The Globe Pequot
Press, 1999). Also more than you'll ever need to know, but
nonetheless an excellent reference, providing you can navigate a
course through the formulas and great detail.

Dowd, John, *Sea Kayaking: Manual for Long Distance Touring* (University
of Washington Press, 1988). Another British-leaning (Canadian)
classic.

Hutchinson, Derek, *The Complete Book of Sea Kayaking* (The Globe
Pequot Press, 1998). An excellent resource, this is the revised
edition of Sir Derek's 1974 classic, *Sea Canoeing* (the first
comprehensive manual about sea kayaking) and is part of the
sport's canon and required reading for literate sea kayakers.

Washburne, Randel, *Coastal Kayaker's Manual* (The Globe Pequot
Press, 1998). A fine New World effort by a Washington-based
paddler, so it's great on tides and currents. A good book to
balance out the Brit perspective.

Other Kayak Instruction Books

Harrison, David, *Hearst Marine Books Sea Kayaking Basics* (William
Morrow & Co., 1993).

Seidman, David, *The Essential Sea Kayaker* (International Marine
Publishing, 1991).

Stuhaug, Dennis, *Kayaking Made Easy* (The Globe Pequot Press, 1998).

Wyatt, Michael (recently updated and edited by Roger Schumann and
Jan Shriner), *The Basic Essentials of Sea Kayaking* (The Globe Pequot
Press, 1999).

All four are designed to be "user-friendly" and nontechnical for beginners, but more advanced-level paddlers may find them not as pithy as the "classics."

Marine Weather

Lilly, Kenneth Jr., *Marine Weather Handbook: Northern & Central California* (Paradise Cay Yacht Sales). Full of general marine weather information, it is an especially relevant resource for Bay Area paddlers.

Classic Kayak Adventure Literature

Brower, Kenneth, *Starship and Canoe* (Harper and Row, 1983). Paddling philosophy of George Dyson's odyssey down the "inside passage" in a homemade *baidarka*.

Broze, Matt and George Gronseth, *Sea Kayaker's Deep Trouble* (McGraw-Hill, 1997). This compilation of accident reports from *Sea Kayaker* magazine should be mandatory reading for all paddlers. Excellent!

Dyson, George, *Baidarka* (Graphic Arts Center Publishing Co., 1994). History and lore of kayaks.

Kane, Joe, *Running the Amazon* (Vintage Books, 1990). Finely crafted account of the first descent of the Amazon, from the Andes to the Atlantic.

Sutherland, Audrey, *Paddling My Own Canoe* (University of Hawaii Press, 1978). Classic adventure tale of an amazing paddler.

Natural History Books

A Natural History of the Monterey Bay National Marine Sanctuary (Monterey Bay Aquarium Press, 1997). This book was written by a team of contributing authors (that included Gordon, Silberstein, and Campbell) under the umbrella of the Monterey Bay Aquarium. Excellent reading on general information for the area.

Evens, Jules G., *The Natural History of the Point Reyes Peninsula* (Point Reyes National Seashore Association, 1993). Comprehensive reading on the National Seashore and beyond.

Gordon, Burton L., *Monterey Bay Area: Natural History and Cultural Imprints* (The Boxwood Press, 1996). Extremely readable and informative.

Henson, Paul and Donald J. Usner, *The Natural History of Big Sur* (University of California Press, 1996). Solid information for most of the Central California coast.

LeBoeuf, Burney J. and Stephanie Kaza, eds., *The Natural History of Año Nuevo* (The Boxwood Press, 1985). Substantial text on a distinct place.

Silberstein, Mark and Eileen Campbell, *Elkhorn Slough* (Monterey Bay Aquarium, 1989). Clear and simple recognition of California's second-largest marine wetland.

Magazines

Canoe and Kayak. Occasional good sea kayaking articles; lots about canoeing and the latest in gear.

Paddler. American Canoe Association slant but generic to paddlesport.

Sea Kayaker. Cutting edge and specific to sea kayaking.

Videos

Brown, Gordon. *OVER—and OUT.* A highly entertaining look at mostly outdated rescue techniques. Excellent section on wet exits and bow rescues, but overall sloppy technique.

Ford, Kent. *Performance Sea Kayaking.* Good visual resource with American Canoe Association (ACA) instructors demonstrating modern stroke and rescue technique.

Holman, Larry. *Sea Kayaking Getting Started.* Similar to the Ford video, but perhaps not as crisply edited. Interesting for its use of well-known Bay Area locations and instructors.

Lull, John. *Surf Kayaking Fundamentals.* An in-depth, no-frills look at surf zone skills. The best single resource on the subject.

Tsunami Rangers. *Kayak Magic.* Entertaining footage of high-impact rock gardens, sea caves, and surf zones. Do not try this at home, kids!

Appendix B

Lessons, Tours, and Rentals

This is a list of companies that we are aware of in operation that offer kayak tours, rentals, and/or classes. This does not imply our endorsement of all of the owners or their staffs for professionalism or safety. We suggest that you contact them directly and ask questions like the following: How long have you been in business? Or, if I sign up for a tour or class, will I be able to get information about the experience or certification of my guide or instructor? Also ask them to describe their range of services and send you a brochure. As of this year, those that we know that have at least one American Canoe Association certified instructors are Blue Waters, Monterey Bay Kayaks, Tamal Saka, Pacific Currents, California Canoe and Kayak, Great Expeditions, Kayak Connection, Central Coast Kayaks, and Eskape (that would be us, last but not least). The list gives only the location(s) of the company's home base even though many run trips up and down the coast.

The Lost Coast and Mendocino

Adventure Rents, Gualala Hotel Plaza; (707) 884–4386 or (888) 881–4FUN

Catch a Canoe and Bicycles, Too!, Big River; (707) 937–0273; *www.standordinn.com*

Dive Crazy Adventures, Albion River; (707) 937–3079 or (707) 925–6214; no rentals available

Force 10, Elk; (707) 877–3505

Lost Coast Kayaking, mobile operation at Van Damme State Beach most weekends in summer; (707) 937–2434

North Coast Adventures, Trinidad; (707) 677–3124; *www.northcoastadventures.com*

Russian River Kayak & Cycle, Monte Rio; (707) 865–2141

Point Reyes National Seashore and Vicinity

Blue Waters, Inverness; (415) 669–2600; *www.bwkayak.com*

Paddlebirding, Stinson Beach; (415) 868–2302; no rentals available

Tamal Saka, Marshall; (415) 663–1743; *www.tamalsaka.com*

San Francisco Bay

Cal Adventures, Berkeley; (510) 642–4000;
  www.calbears.berkeley.edu/recsports/scra/caladv/seakayak

California Canoe and Kayak, Oakland; (510) 893–7833 and Pillar Point
  Harbor; (415) 728–1803; *www.calkayak.com*

Current Adventures, Palo Alto; (530) 642–9755 or (888) 4–KAYAKING

Outdoors Unlimited, San Francisco; (415) 476–2078;
  www.outdoors.ucsf.edu/ou

Riptides & Rapids, Mountain View; (650) 961–1240

Sea Trek, Sausalito; (415) 488–1000; *www.seatrekkayak.com*

Monterey Bay Marine Sanctuary and Vicinity

A B Seas Kayaking, Monterey; (831) 647–0147; *www.kayak.idsite.com*

Adventure Sports, Santa Cruz; (831) 458–3648; *www.asudoit.com*

Adventures by the Sea, Monterey; (831) 372–1807;
  www.adventuresbythesea.com

Eskape Sea Kayaking, Santa Cruz; (831) 427–2297; *www.eskapekayak.com*

Great Expeditions, Santa Cruz; (831) 425–0390;
  www.premierline.com/great-expeditions

Kayak Connection, Santa Cruz; (831) 479–1121 and Moss Landing;
  (831) 724–5692; *www.cruzio.com/~laualcpm*

Monterey Bay Kayaks, Monterey; (831) 373–5357;
  www.montereykayaks.com

Venture Quest, Santa Cruz; (831) 427–2267;
  www.members.cruzio.com/~venture/

Big Sur Coast to Morro Bay

Central Coast Kayaks, Shell Beach; (805) 773–3500;
  www.centralcoastkayaks.com

Good Clean Fun, Cayucos; (805) 995–1993

Kayak Horizons, Morro Bay; (805) 772–6444

Index